FR WERENFRIED

FR WERENFRIED
–A LIFE

JOANNA BOGLE

Gracewing.

First published in 2001

Gracewing
2 Southern Avenue, Leominster
Herefordshire HR6 0QF

ISBN 0 85244 479 6

We are grateful for permission to reproduce the following copyright
photographs in the plate section:
To Martien Coppens – p. 2, p. 3 (second photograph), and p. 8;
KNA-Bild – p. 4; Andrej Polec – pp. 7, 14 and 15; Felici – p. 13;
L'Osservatore Romano – p. 16 (first photograph); Balz Röthlin –
p. 16 (second photograph). All other photographic material has been
supplied by Aid to the Church in Need.

Typeset by
Action Publishing Technology Ltd, Gloucester GL1 5SR

Printed by
MPG Books Ltd., Bodmin PL31 1EG

FOREWORD

by Neville Kyrke-Smith

I sat with Father Werenfried in a side chapel at Westminster Cathedral in London. He was about to preach, but wanted me to go over his pronunciation with him – he did not want a word to be lost amongst the two thousand who had gathered to hear him. At this same Rosary Crusade, in October 1993, a volunteer was standing with many others at the back of the Cathedral when some tourists squeezed their way in. 'Hey, look there!' the man said. 'There's someone in white preaching up there.' 'Yes,' said his wife, mishearing the accent, 'I think it's the Pope.' Then they stayed to listen.

Well, the Pope he was not – but Father Werenfried always spoke and wrote with authority. His challenging Catholicism continually inspired or provoked people. He prepared his talks, sermons and letters with meticulous care. Never held back by cowardice or fear of how some people might react, he would preach 'in season and out of season'. His was not a fair-weather Christianity, but a challenging presentation of the Way of the Cross and the hope of the Resurrection. Somehow, through his letters in the *Mirror* newsletter, he united the generous benefactors – their concerns and all they endured – with the beneficiaries, in all they suffered for following Christ. The apostolate of the charity he founded, Aid to the Church in Need, was founded on the spirit of this remarkable man.

Foreword

'I am no saint,' Father Werenfried would protest. And this lively and open book reflects that this beggar for God was a real human being – with humour, failings, frustrations and a sometimes-irascible manner. Yet he was a visionary of the Catholic Church in the late twentieth century, who often went where angels fear to tread. He had the audacity to appeal for aid to help German refugees from those who had suffered appallingly at their hands. He said that we must have a community of Sisters to pray for the faithful and all those who died at Auschwitz. He stood up against an Ostpolitik that accepted that Communism would last forever and therefore we had to accommodate the Church accordingly. He preached and wrote against the sad abuses and misuse of 'the spirit of Vatican II' in liturgical and moral spheres. In later years, he once again appealed for reconciliation – this time between East and West – in asking Catholics to help their Orthodox brothers and sisters in the East.

The vision of Father Werenfried lives on in the work of Aid to the Church in Need – and his demanding words will echo across the world as the Catholic charity continues to respond to the needs of those who are still being persecuted for their faith today, and of those in real pastoral need: 'They are being tested in faith. We are being tested in love.' I am sure that every reader will be inspired by this book, written by the author and journalist Joanna Bogle who has known Werenfried for over thirty years. Reading about his life, perhaps we can hear again Werenfried's call for inner conversion. For his was a mission of love – love for Christ, His Church and His people. He had no time for a liberal understanding of love, and could not cope with lukewarm Christianity. His simple question came from God – are you for Me or against Me?

Invoking Our Lady, Father Werenfried would often conclude his homilies in a similar way – saying, 'I would give up the whole of today's collection if just one young man here would decide to become a priest, or one young woman decide to become a nun.' Then he would look up, as though to heaven, and ask people to prepare for the day when they would meet our Mother, echoing the prayer to Our Lady of Fatima. May his prayer be said for each one of us and for him:

Mother, now that the need is at its greatest and the powers of darkness seem to have free rein, we come to you with childlike trust and implore your powerful aid. Now, swept away and rudderless on the tempest of this age, we place ourselves, together with the whole of disfigured humanity and our organisation of the Church in need, in your maternal hands. We consecrate ourselves to you, dear Virgin of Fatima. Preserve us in the love of your Son, protect us from the evil of this world and lead us safe to the heart of God. And grant, dear Mother, when we have passed through death's dark gate and stand before the Judgement Seat of your Son, that we may find you there with a smile in your eyes, and be able to say without fear: 'Here we are, Mother.'

Neville Kyrke-Smith
National Director of
Aid to the Church in Need, UK

Chapter One

The story of Father Werenfried has its real origins in a tragedy at the end of the nineteenth century in a farming family in Hagestein, Holland.

A farmer named van Straaten was the devoted father of eight children, including four sons. His first wife had died and some years later he had married a second time. The van Straatens were a devout and loving Catholic family, moderately prosperous, and lived in a traditional farming-based community not far from Amsterdam. As the three eldest boys – sons of the first marriage – grew up, they gradually took over the running of the farm. The youngest boy, Evert, born in 1881, was more quiet and studious, and was set on being a priest. These were serene years and it must have seemed to the van Straatens that their way of life would continue unchanged for ever. But in the year 1890 tragedy struck. A massive typhoid epidemic ravaged the countryside, moving swiftly from family to family and bringing death in its wake.

The three eldest van Straaten boys all caught the disease and within one week all three were dead. The desolated parents – themselves no longer young – saw the end of all their family happiness. Their youngest son knew that his life, too, had changed for ever. He could no longer become a priest. As the sole male breadwinner now left in the family, he must work to support his elderly parents. He renounced his plans to study in the seminary, and instead became a teacher. Although he worked hard and appeared to enjoy his job, he had found the decision to give up the plans for the priesthood a very hard one to make. Privately he prayed that, if he married and had a family, he would have a son who would become a priest.

In due course Evert met and married a fellow teacher, Catharina – full name Catharina Carolina Johanna van Hove – and they settled in the small town of Mijdrecht. The first daughter was baptised Ina. Sadly, she died while still very young. When another daughter came, she was baptised Antonia, a family name which had been held by several generations. There were three boys – Gerard, Philip and Johan. Evert's elderly mother came to live with the family. They were a close-knit and affectionate team, with the children forming strong bonds with one another. Evert continued to pray that he would have a son who would be a priest and his prayers were answered in an extraordinary way. Each of his three boys discovered that he had a priestly vocation.

The second son, Philip Johannes Hendrick, was born on 11 January 1913. He slotted cheerfully into place in a family where the Catholic faith, a cheerful commitment to hard work, and plenty of affection, formed the background to life. The name Philip means 'a lover of horses', but although a country boy, he never had any particular interest in riding. When he grew up he would be given another name – Werenfried – 'a fighter for peace'. It was with that name that he would become famous.

Philip and his brothers grew up in Mijdrecht, today part of the suburbs of Amsterdam but then a small town in its own right. His first years were dominated by the Great War, and as the fighting ended his family was one of the many caught up in the epidemic of Spanish Influenza which took so many lives that the war had spared. The small Philip recovered from the disease – the first of many serious illnesses which were to dog his life – and in November 1919 was ready to go to school. This was Helmond, where his father was then teaching. Then in January 1920 his father was posted to another school at Leeuwarden – but influenza there forced the family back to the country near Eindhoven. Philip was an intelligent boy and seemed likely to go on to university.

Already his two brothers, Johan and Gerard, had made it clear that they wanted to be priests, and had chosen the Augustinian order, the religious institute basing its way of life on the Rule of St Augustine. This was an unusual choice, in that the Augustinians had a reputation for being somewhat strict. It was in fact the religious order to which Martin Luther had belonged, and from which he had rebelled to start the Reformation. Now Gerard joined, taking the name Modestus, and was later followed by Johan who took the name Amatus. When they next made visits home, they were wearing the full-length black habit of the Augustinian order, and conscious of being part of a heritage stretching back many hundreds of years.

Looking back later, their younger brother stated with honesty 'I frankly felt that two priests was enough for one family.' Johan and Gerard had both shown early signs of a desire to give themselves to God as priests. They had both played, as small boys, at celebrating Masses, erecting small altars and carefully mimicking what they had seen in church on Sundays. Small Philip would be roped in to act as an altar server. As a teenager he got tired of it all and developed rather anti-religious views. It was with a determination to be independent and to make his own decisions that, in 1932, he set off for Utrecht University.

Evert van Straaten worked hard to pay the fees for his

sons at university – giving private correspondence lessons in the evenings to people who wanted to learn English, French, and German. He had high hopes for Philip, who was studying classics – perhaps he might even become a professor.

Philip had initially wanted to be a painter. But he also developed a love of discussing politics and social issues. He became involved in a crusading group which was challenging various ideas within the Church, and he also founded a political party – although it was a rather typically student venture and had a short lifespan.

Philip's brothers were concerned about him. He seemed to have ideas at variance with those officially approved by the then rather straight-laced Dutch bishops. He had friends who were definitely opposed to the Church. His earlier cynicism about religious matters developed a cutting edge and he became quite a dedicated anti-clerical. (He was a man born before his time – half a century later, the Dutch bishops were to become famous for permitting and even encouraging many teachings wholly at variance with Catholic doctrine.)

A priest who very much inspired Philip was Father Raymond van Sante, who fell foul of the Dutch bishops and eventually had to leave the country and settle in Germany.

The group he founded in Utrecht played a big part in Philip's life – not only with discussion and ideas but with practical social action including visiting the elderly and sick and running amateur theatricals. Political idealism matched the eagerness for social action: the political group which Philip helped to found had a message of 'National Solidarity' and was opposed to both the Communists and to the emerging National Socialists, who were coming to power in neighbouring Germany.

All this meant that he had a very full life. But what did the future hold, and where was everything leading?

In later years, writing about this period, he was never able to explain properly just what happened. His vocation seems to have come almost as a bolt from the blue. Although he was to spend much of his life writing, preaching and teaching with immense passion about religious things, and to draw many people into a deeper relationship with God, about his own spiritual journey he always remained reticent.

'To everyone's amazement God called me to the religious life in 1934,' he said starkly. 'Although at that very moment I was head over heels in love. The sacrifice that was asked of me cost me more than I can write ... If I had stopped to think about it I would probably have said no. But it is not my habit to think long about things and I had the temerity to say yes.'

Who was the young lady with whom he was in love? She was a friend of the family, whom Philip had known for years. He hadn't yet spoken to her about his true feelings, but for some while there had not been much doubt in his mind. She would make a perfect wife. But then came this different and unmistakeable call.

Initially, and with the fervour of a newly-discovered Christian radicalism, he wanted to join the Capuchins. But they were an austere order and Philip's health was not good. They told him firmly that he would not be able to endure their harsh life with its poor diet. So he had to look elsewhere. His search took him away from his native Holland to the Norbertine abbey at Tongerlo in neighbouring Belgium.

The Norbertines are a religious order named after their founder St Norbert and also known as Premonstratensians because their original house was at Premontre in France.

St Norbert, who lived in the eleventh century, came from a noble family and entered religious life after a dramatic conversion experience following a narrow escape from death. He founded the Premonstratensians as a community dedicated to prayer, preaching and an active priestly life. He himself travelled extensively as a preacher and was eventually made Bishop of Magdeburg, where his reforming zeal brought clashes with more lax clergy but eventually gave new life to the Church in the whole area.

The legacy of St Norbert was a form of religious life which was both active and contemplative: it meant much time spent in prayer but also a busy programme of preaching and working to change and inspire the lives of ordinary people in towns and parishes. The Norbertines, with their distinctive white robes, became over the centuries a recognised part of Catholic life.

At Tongerlo, the young men were trained for hard working lives. They were urged to live austerely, to spend much time in prayer, not to consider their own comfort, and to dedicate their whole lives to God and the Church. Philip plunged into this with enthusiasm. Entering the monastery meant a radical break with everything that had gone before. It meant new clothes – from now on, he would wear an ankle-length long-sleeved white robe, with a wide belt and a shoulder-cape. It marked him out as a uniform marks a soldier. And with all this came a new routine, a whole new approach – and a new name, symbolising the fresh commitment that had been made. Philip became Werenfried. It was by this name that he would be known for the rest of his life.

A fellow monk was later to remember: 'He was very skinny and didn't look very well. He was also very ascetic, he didn't eat much and he tried to live as moderately as he could. But being a student, he was already involved with all kinds of activities.'

Typically, he overdid things. He fasted with such dedication that he became ill. A doctor, called in to make a report, stated categorically that he was too frail for missionary work, routine parish work, or preaching. Since these were the main activities of the Norbertines, it seemed that Werenfried would have to be sent back home. But Abbot Stalmans at Tongerlo knew that he had a dedicated if somewhat over-zealous young novice who had much to offer. He announced that there was a place for Werenfried as a choir-monk. The young man's vocation was saved and he was able to remain in the Abbey and be ordained. His actual musical contribution to the Abbey's choir was large in enthusiasm but rather more modest in talent – he sang loudly, cheerfully, and slightly out of tune.

Abbot Stalmans was to be a loyal and fatherly support to Werenfried over many years. Werenfried would often tell of the Abbot's long-suffering patience summed up in the comment 'I'm very glad to have Werenfried ... But I'm also glad that there's only one Werenfried.'

On 25 July 1940, Werenfried was ordained a priest. From now on, he would celebrate Mass every day of his life, and the fact of his priesthood would define him, being the central reality behind everything that he would do or write.

His entry into the monastery had not meant a break with his family – on the contrary, they remained close and affectionate, and this was to continue down the years. He kept up with the family news, and with news of friends. (It was through this that he heard, about a year after his ordination, one particularly sad item – the young lady with whom he had once been in love had been taken seriously ill and died.)

These were all years of war. As Werenfried had been

preparing for ordination, in the outside world events had been moving swiftly, with Holland and Belgium invaded by the Germans. His priesthood began in an occupied country, in a Europe torn by a war that would last for five more years.

Among Werenfried's old university friends, there were some who wore Allied uniforms and fought passionately against the Germans, and others who genuinely believed that Germany was right and that sense could be made of a New Order in Europe. Among those who had shared his discussions about National Solidarity in the university days in Utrecht, there were some who joined the Dutch underground to fight the Germans, and others who believed that perhaps the future lay with supporting the German National Socialists.

For a monk living in an occupied country, the war years must have been a time of frustration and anxiety. As a Catholic priest Werenfried had to believe in solutions that lay beyond the immediate battles. He was later to write about it:

> I was between two fires as I could not interpret the hideous slaughter as anything else but a conflict among heathens for the things of this world. In a country groaning under enemy occupation I held forth that Christians are supposed to love their enemies ... I had friends among the Communists and in the German army, among quislings, in the Resistance and among the volunteers who were fighting on the eastern front against the Russians. This often got me into difficulties. Almost all who were personally engaged were convinced that their homeland, Europe, God, a New Order or all other ideals could only be served in one way – the way they thought right themselves.

As the war ended, he was able along with so many others to list the toll of the friends he had lost. Some had gone to German concentration camps and never returned. Others had been killed in British or American bombing raids. Others had been soldiers, sailors and airmen killed in uniform – and he had friends on both sides.

Meanwhile a great tide of suffering humanity was now on the move across Europe as post-war negotiations redrew the map of the continent. How would Christianity respond to the colossal needs of this new era? How were the hungry to be fed, the vast numbers of the homeless and refugees given shelter? How could former enemies be reconciled? What were the chances of a genuine and lasting peace in a century which had seen two bitter wars within twenty years of each other? Could any sort of Christian ideals and culture survive with Soviet Communism bearing down from the East, and bitter hardship and misery as the daily reality for millions in the heart of the continent?

It was in responding to these questions that Werenfried van Straaten was to find his life's mission.

Chapter Two

In June 1944, the Allied armies invaded mainland Europe and the bitter fighting of the last months of the war began. By September 1944 the Germans had been beaten back out of Belgium, and as far as that country was concerned the war was over and their land was free again. The monks at Tongerlo, along with their fellow country-men, faced the gigantic task of restoring a wounded and battered nation.

But when the peace treaties were finally signed, the massive wave of refugees struggling across the frontiers of a broken and starving continent was beyond anything that had ever been seen in history. Under the treaties of Yalta and Potsdam which redrew the map of Europe, a total of fourteen million Germans were uprooted from their homes and lands in territory that was now to be allo-cated to Poland and Czechoslovakia – nations which themselves were to be re-formed under new systems and dominated as satellite states by the Soviet Union.

This is a whole chapter of human misery which, because it occurred at the end of a world war which had seen so much slaughter, has tended to be overlooked by histori-ans. In the new map of Central and Eastern Europe, Poland was moved sharply westward and much of her former eastern territory allocated to the Soviet satellite state of Ukraine. The creation of the 'Communist bloc' of nations was the primary fruit of the Second World War as far as the USSR was concerned, and a major achievement of Stalin, the Soviet leader.

The conference at Yalta in the Crimea in 1945 brought together the rulers of the three main Allied nations: President Roosevelt of America, Prime Minister Winston Churchill of Britain, and the Soviet leader Stalin. Poland, the country first invaded by Nazi Germany, was not represented at the conference – her territory had already been taken by the advancing Soviet forces and a puppet form of government had been created under them. The Polish government had been exiled in Britain throughout the war years and was now anxious to return home – but decisions were being made which would make that impossible.

After defining the borders of a new Poland, the Yalta Conference turned to the question of the people already living in the territories concerned – the German population which now had to leave. It all seemed quite simple and could be tackled in an orderly manner:

The three Governments (ie British, American, and Soviet), having considered the question in all its aspects, recognize that the transfer to Germany of German populations or elements thereof remaining in Poland, Czechoslovakia and Hungary, will have to be undertaken. They agree that any transfers that take place should be effected in an orderly and humane manner.

Since the influx of large numbers of Germans into Germany would increase the burden already resting on the occupying authorities, they consider that the Allied Control Council in Germany should in the first instance examine the problem with special regard to the question of the equitable distribution of those Germans about the several zones of occupation ...[1]

But of course the reality of transferring large numbers of people across a continent already devastated by war was not going to be orderly or humane at all – and as these people were Germans, from a nation which had started the war and through its Nazi ideology had imposed horror, murder and evil wherever it had ruled, there was not to be much pity for them or much material aid put at their disposal.

Thus while in Britain and elsewhere people were relishing the end of bombing raids and the black-out, coping with the continuing food rationing and fuel shortages, thrilling to new musicals such as *Oklahoma!* and enjoying the prospect of the Royal Wedding of the young Princess Elizabeth, elsewhere in Europe things were rather different. In the East, refugees were hungry, homeless, destitute and lacking in any hope.

Understandably, most people in the free world, themselves exhausted after the years of war, were busy with their own post-war hopes and work and plans. Their men were coming home – some from horrific experiences in Japanese prisoner-of-war camps, or wounded after desert battles. The newspapers were starting to advertise a few luxury goods. It became possible to go on holiday again, to visit the seaside, now freed from barbed wire and concrete tank-traps.

Few people in the English-speaking world wanted to hear about destitute Germans. If they did read about it, the comment would probably be 'Well, they had it coming to them'. Germans were simply the people who had started the war, and not much else about them was of interest to most British people as the war ended.

The German refugees were from whole stretches of Europe where their families had lived and farmed for hundreds of years. The German port of Danzig (now Gdansk in Poland) was one place from where many tried to get to the West as the Soviet Army advanced in the last stages of the war – huge numbers died on one ship which left heading westwards and was sunk, creating the world's worst-ever shipping disaster. With the signing of the final peace treaties, the disaster worsened: millions of Germans now had to leave and could head nowhere except westwards, where they would have to camp out in the ruined cities and old air-raid bunkers where the people of a broken and defeated German Reich were struggling to live and where there was a lack of the most fundamental necessities of food and shelter.

The actual status of defeated Germany had been spelled out in the statement by the governments of Britain, America, the USSR and the provisional government of France in the earliest days of victory in June 1945:

Germany, with her frontiers as they were on 31 December 1937, will, for the purposes of occupation, be divided into four zones, one to be allotted to each Power as follows:

an eastern zone to the Union of Soviet Socialist Republics;
a north-western zone to the United Kingdom;
a south-western zone to the United States of America;
a western zone to France.

The occupying forces in each zone will be under a Commander-in-Chief designated by the responsible Power ... The area of 'Greater Berlin' [ie the city which had been the capital of the former German Reich, together with some of its surrounding suburbs] will be occupied by forces of each of the four Powers. An Inter-Allied Governing Authority consisting of four Commandants, appointed by their respective Commanders-in-Chief, will be established to direct jointly its administration.[2]

The drift westward of the Germans from the territories that were now to be Poland and the new Czechoslovakia had begun before the war ended, as people fled from the advancing Red Army. Many families were split up in the chaos, as war had already driven them apart and now there was no settled home or point of reference.

By 1945 thousands of German soldiers remained unaccounted for after the battles against the Soviet Union: large numbers were dead or were dying in the labour camps of the Gulag. The Soviet Union had not signed the Geneva Convention regarding the treatment of prisoners-of-war and so did not feel bound in any way to treat prisoners with mercy. Names of those who had survived battles such as Stalingrad were not released – and letters to and from the labour camps were of course impossible. Families, themselves uprooted and homeless, knew that they might never know the fate of a husband, father, or brother. (In fact it was not until 1955 – ten years after the end of the war, that the then Chancellor Konrad Adenauer, leader of the newly-created republic of West Germany, was able to get to Russia and successfully plead with the Soviet leaders for the return of the surviving prisoners.)

While the Germans expelled from Eastern Europe obviously had few friends or sympathisers among the victorious nations, their plight was of concern to the

Church, the one institution which must always be concerned with the unfortunate, even if they also happen to be the disdained and the unpopular. It was from Rome that the first requests came to Fr Werenfried's abbey at Tongerlo that something might be done for the expellees – and initially specifically for the priests who were among them and who were the effective leaders of the displaced people. The request went to the energetic young Fr Werenfried, who always seemed eager for any new initiative and whose brain always seemed to be tumbling with the ideas and enterprises that had first begun in student days and were only marginally tamed by abbey life.

Encouraged by his abbot, Werenfried wrote an appeal for help for the German expellees, tugging at the heartstrings of the people of Flanders among whom he lived. They were country people, traditional-minded Catholics, generous, patriotic, and thrifty. They had suffered in the war, and knew what it was to live in anxiety and fear. They also knew their Catholic faith, and were aware that it taught about loving enemies, sharing food with the poor and hungry, and being ultimately judged by God for all deeds performed while on this earth. Slowly at first, and then eventually in great numbers, they responded to the call of the priest from the abbey of Tongerlo, and began to collect together food and clothes which could be sent to the camps and the areas of Germany to where the displaced refugees were being sent.

Because it is important first to establish the background to this massive expellee relief scheme which was the beginning of Fr Werenfried's international work, it is necessary to explain just what the displacement of four-teen million Germans from Eastern Europe was like.

Father Werenfried was soon to come to know many of the expellees personally, especially the priests. He heard at first-hand their accounts of fleeing from the Soviet Army, and of what it had been like being in that army's path as it made its sweep westwards across Eastern Europe in the last months of the war:

When after the arrival of the Soviet troops or during the orgies that everywhere accompanied the liberation from enemy yoke, slaughter and rape were the order of the day, these priests remained like good shepherds with their flocks. It can be understood that when the Soviets first occupied a village or a town they first vented their rage on the head of the priest. From numerous reports we learned that hundreds of them were shot down for defending women and girls who had sought refuge in the presbytery. Often a parish priest was the only one to defend nuns, girls and even children when threatened with assault by drunken troops. Many also at the cost of their own lives tried to prevent the desecration of sacred places. Frequently the Russians did not dare to murder the priest in public but first enticed him out of the convent or presbytery to a deserted spot. His mutilated corpse was then only found some weeks or months later.

There were only very few priests in the evacuation areas who escaped death or were not in danger or maltreated. And these survivors who had already drunk to the very dregs the overflowing chalice of human suffering remained with their flocks when the decrees of the Russian, British and American authorities at Yalta and Potsdam to expel 16 million Germans from their century-old homelands were carried out in the most inhuman manner. Very often they were the sole leaders of the expelled who were driven in endless transports to the West.[3]

In 1946, 1947 and 1948, the refugee disaster threatened to overwhelm all attempts to create some sort of order in the chaos of post-war Germany. The territories into which the refugees were fleeing were themselves destitute – and dismantling of the few remaining industries was proceeding apace under the system agreed by the victorious Allies for controlling any German industrial production.

In November 1945 the Allied Control Council in Germany had announced its plans:

> 1. The entire German population to be moved from Poland (three and a half million persons) will be admitted to the Soviet and British zones of occupation in Germany.
> 2. The entire German population to be moved from Czechoslovakia, Austria and Hungary (3,150,000 persons) will be admitted to the American, French and Soviet occupation zones of Germany.[4]

There followed statistics detailing the numbers of Germans to be transported and accepted into the various zones over the next months. By February 1946 some of this was in operation:

> Expellees will be accepted by the British authorities on the border of Poland and the Soviet Occupied Zone of Germany, and, for this purpose, British Repatriation Teams will be stationed at Stettin and Kalawsk (Kohlfurt). Agreed that trainloads and shipments having been inspected and approved by British Repatriation Teams in Polish territory will be accepted without question by the British Zone authorities. This is to ensure that trainloads will not be turned back into Soviet Occupied Zone of Germany ...

> All expellees will be dusted with DDT Powder at
> Stettin and Kalawsk which will be observed by the
> British Repatriation Teams ... Expellees will be
> permitted to take with them as much of their own
> baggage as they can carry in their hands, including
> bedding and cooking utensils ...[5]

Meanwhile, massive differences were already emerging
between the Allied Powers, with the beginning of what
was to develop into the Cold War, which was to dominate
Europe for the next half-century. The final official borders
of Poland, the nature and extent of war reparations from
Germany (the dismantling of factories and the sending of
the parts to Russia to build new industries there), the
establishment of a new currency for the Germans to use
... all these created ever-widening divisions between the
Western Allies and the Soviets. German refugees,
together with the Germans already living in the four
different zones – and all the refugees of other nationalities
who were still teeming in Europe as people sought to find
their old homes or make new ones – were people squeezed
in the middle.

Coping with refugees, and building new communities
for the future, could not be something left to governments. Ordinary people had to help each other – and the
Church had to be at the heart of this. It was the only way
ahead.

Werenfried listened to the information about the plight
of the expellees and took on the project with the enthusiasm he had brought to everything else he had done in life.
When he was able to visit Germany and see for himself
the horrors of a starving and destitute former enemy, he
was stirred as never before. It was not only the hunger,
deprivation, and misery, but also the moral squalour that

appalled the visitor – the camps were filled with people who were being robbed of all hope, who had lost those dearest to them and the homes that had given meaning, purpose and structure to life.

The expelled Germans, sent to various parts of Germany, ended up in a number of different situations. Some were in camps, or in the temporary shelter provided by vast air-raid shelters. Others were sent to rural areas where they lived as best they could among the local population. Some went to centres where they were later to be joined by other refugees – people fleeing from what was now to be the Soviet-dominated block of Eastern Europe.

Fr Werenfried himself explained how he came to be involved with aid to these refugees, and the defeated nation into which they were pouring:

'In September '44, after the war was over in Belgium, our general at that time, Monsignor Noots, came from Rome to my abbot and said that the Pope – that was Pius XII – asked me to undertake some action in Belgium for the exiled German priests. And then in 1946, according to the treaties of Yalta and Potsdam, 14 million Germans were exiled to completely Protestant regions of Germany – among them were 3000 priests and 6 million Catholics. So I went to Germany ...'

In fact Fr Werenfried's first appeal came as a result of a well-known Dutch radio preacher, Fr Henri de Greeve. It was December 1947 and Fr Werenfried was writing an article for the Christmas edition of the Abbey's magazine. In it, he drew on the fact that the German border was only a fairly short distance away, and – using partly the descriptions provided by Fr de Greeve and others – he brought alive the reality of existence there:

'Eighty miles to the east lies a town in ruins. Hardly anything remains of it except a gigantic air-raid shelter, a

so-called bunker, like the ones the Germans built everywhere to protect the population from bombing. Those of
the impoverished people of the town who still remain
alive dwell in this single bunker. Thousands are crowded
together in pestilential stench. Each family, in so far as
they can still be called families, lies huddled together on a
few square yards of concrete. Here is neither fire nor
warmth, other than the warmth of bodies crowded
together. Among these people, too, Christ seeks to dwell
in His purity, His love and goodness. The shepherds
worshipped Christ in a stable, but these people have not
even a stable. By human standards Christ cannot live
there. There is no room for Him ...'

That first Christmas appeal opened many hearts – and
purses and wallets – and aid for the defeated Germans
began to flow. In later years, Fr Werenfried would date the
launch of what was to become Aid to the Church in Need
from that first Christmas letter. He always recalled that in
fact he wrote it late into the night, and the clock was
actually striking 3 a.m. when he put the final words on
paper.

A few months later, Fr Werenfried was on his way to
Germany himself. Travel in those first post-war months
and years was not easy, but this trip was arranged through
a Franciscan, Fr Valerius Claes, who had formed a group
calling for 'Catholic unity' and appealing for brotherly
help for German Catholics.

'Never shall I forget the impression made on me by the
visit to a Hochbunker. Black and square rose the
monstrous building against the bright summer sky. A
dark block of concrete, as large as a factory, with two
gaping mouths, like the god of destruction reigning over
all the ruins of Germany, it was the modern Moloch to
which the helpless children of our times were sacrificed,

the new beast threatening Christianity. In the very place where the churches had been swept away by the war, these monsters had remained standing. Black as the night they devoured hundreds of thousands of those who, by the terms of the Decree of Potsdam, were doomed to exile.'

Once he got home, he wrote a passionate appeal to the people of Flanders. If the first Christmas letter had seemed dramatic – and had certainly produced some criticisms from people who said he was being too sympathetic to the Germans – this one was to do much more.

Describing the bunker as a 'beast of prey' he invited readers to travel with him into its entrails, to smell the stench of decay and hopelessness that filled it:

'What a black page in the history of the Church! Here the outcast Christians are huddled together in nakedness and squalour. Four families chosen at random are cast into each concrete cave. Sixteen beds or more fill the available space. There is no room for tables and chairs. Nowhere any homeliness or family life. No privacy. Everywhere lustful eyes, lewd gestures, indecent talk, wanton laughter. There is no protection against all this. Living in herds destroys all sense of decency.

'Here families with four, five, or six children gradually waste away, sallow, shrivelled babies as well as grand-mothers of eighty, in an oppressive stench of sweat and fetid air. There are no windows. For years there was nothing more than the sooty light of candles and torches. There are no lamps. But those who live here long develop weak eyes and can no longer bear the sunlight. Consumptives spit in a basin. Old people in their dotage wallow in their own filth. Children crawl under the beds, in the narrow passages and up and down the concrete staircases. These anaemic children are dreadful to see –

pale and transparent, with precocious eyes and a piteous smile on their aged faces.'

Fr Werenfried noted sadly that the question most frequently asked by the refugees was 'When are we going home?' They had come from East Prussia or from Silesia, from farms where golden cornfields flanked roads that led to villages dominated by baroque churches. They could not believe that, as Germans, they were simply banned from these territories that they regarded as their home-land, where their families had lived and farmed for generations. But these lands were now being given over to Czechs or to Poles. (Ironically, some of the Czechs would later flee in their turn to West Germany, because of the terror unleashed by the new Communist authorities in their land – a situation which would cause tension in some of the camps where they were given shelter.)

These early visits to Germany, and the resulting cash collections to provide basic comforts for the people living in the bunkers and camps, marked out a whole new way of life for Werenfried. Given permission by his Abbot to devote himself to this work, he threw himself into relief work which took him across all of Flanders.

'At first, I had to go and find my audience,' he recalled. 'I went to meet them during the lunch hour at the factory gates. I got right into the meetings or tea parties of country guilds and women's institutes. I stood in my white habit on the motorways until a factory owner gave me a lift in his Cadillac so that I could rouse him with my sensational news. I went from school to school to ask for the children's prayers, a piece of chocolate, and the contents of their money-box for the Church in distress.'

Using the Abbey at Tongerlo as his base, he set up a structure that was to provide a mechanism through which aid could be sent direct to Germany. Cash had to be sorted and counted, parcels made up, sweets and clothing packed and delivered. For the refugee priests, who were playing a crucial role in helping their own refugee people, something specific was needed. With the help of his fellow clergy Werenfried launched a system through which Flemish Catholic children, through their schools, adopted priests and sent them letters and parcels. The bond that was forged was personal: the children sent their own handwritten letters, and made up parcels containing food, medicine, sweets for children, and other items. The notion of 'rucksack priests', the priests from the refugee areas, trudging round from camp to camp, consoling and teaching and helping and offering Mass and the Sacraments, became a central feature of what was already now a charity with a status and a name. The name came, indirectly, from Britain's wartime Prime Minister Winston Churchill. At Fulton, Missouri, in a major lecture reviewing the world situation, he said that an 'Iron Curtain' had descended across Europe. Fr Werenfried, helping the refugees who had been caught up in this tragedy, called his charity simply 'Iron Curtain Church Relief'.

It was a picture of one child – the only one of five children to survive forced expulsion from Breslau – that created one of Fr Werenfried's most effective fund-raising tools, and also gave him one of his most extraordinary experiences.

Little 'Rosemarie' was photographed in a German refugee camp by a fellow-worker of Fr Werenfried's, who sent the snapshot to him asking if this child could be helped. Her father was dead. She and her mother alone survived of the whole family, having seen the four other children die one by one. They had reached a camp, but they had nothing – they were being issued with food rations but had no clothes of their own and had left all their family possessions behind as they struggled to Western Germany. Moved by the story, Fr Werenfried arranged for clothes to be sent and added some chocolate and a doll for the little girl. He used her snapshot alongside a letter which was published across Belgium to implore help for all the children like her. Rosemarie was not her real name, but he used it in order to protect her privacy:

Rosemarie, I have never met you, for I only know you from the sad photo that was sent to me. But I know that you live in a camp and that is why you look like a tiny faded flower only fit to be gathered quickly.

I, too, have been in a camp. Not as a refugee and not to live for weeks in an emergency shed. No, I was only there on a visit. To look round. To distribute cigarettes and sweets. To search in vain for a word of comfort and finally just to shake hands and leave despondent.

I tried honestly to do some good there. I held a short address for the refugees. I did not know if it did any good. It certainly did not do any good to Friedhilde, although I talked to her for a whole hour. Yes, I did what I could, but I was not able to convince her. She remained just as hopeless as before. The next morning she was dead, with her wrists cut. Suicide.

That was what it was like when I visited that camp. The rest I can imagine. Life in the family hutments without shame, day and night. The beds one above the other, next to each other and behind each other. For boys and girls, women and children. Anchorless people, uprooted, stateless and without relations, dehumanised and abased to the state of growling, starving animals grabbing and devouring whatever they could claw at.

Annemarie, how old are you? Are you seven years old? That is far too young for hell. Of course the look of surprise has been quenched from your eyes, for there is nothing that has been kept from you. And you have learnt about everything, without glamour, without secrecy, shamelessly and brutally.

Where is your father? Was he murdered in a fight in the camp like the fathers in the Valka-lager at Nuremberg at the rate of two a week? Or is he missing in Russia? Killed in the war? In prison in Siberia? Has he left mother? Has he died of consumption?

Heidemarie, if you had a brave strong father you would not now have to stand so utterly miserable in the porch of this wooden shed! For he would take you on his shoulders and stride away, prancing and singing, far away from here ... to a white cottage with red tiles and blue smoke from the chimney and a snow-white bed to sleep in ...

And your mother? Or do you only have a grand-mother? Or an old aunt? But perhaps you still have your own mother. Maybe she is crying and sick for home. Has her voice now become rough and does she swear at the men? Or did she beat you because you disturbed her behind the worn-out blanket in the corner, with her friend whom you have to call uncle?

Marie-Louise, don't be angry with her, for she is still poorer than you are. Rosemarie, Marie-Louise, Annemarie, Heidemarie, I don't even know what your name is. I just called you that because I would like to entrust all the Roses, Hildas, Annes and all the other little girls in the refugee camps to the Mother of Sorrows, the pure Virgin Mary, who knows why you are so sad. For she, too, had to fly with her child and that is why, with understanding mother-love, she loves all the children in the camp, and also you.

The picture of Rosemarie brought money in from people across Belgium who were now just beginning to prosper as the first hardships of war receded. They did not have very much, but the farming was no longer disrupted by war, and the industries were turning out normal products, and it was possible to have a home life and to buy necessary things – and to give to charity. People began to talk about this vigorous priest who went from parish to parish in his Norbertine habit, stirring consciences and pointing out that a massive refugee problem in the heart of Europe was everybody's problem, not just that of the Germany of the ruling Allied Powers.

Iron Curtain Church Relief was a provocative name. It challenged Christians in Western Europe. It spelled out a sense of responsibility for people on the other side of the curtain. It held out the future possibility that it might even be possible to penetrate the curtain itself.

And what of Rosemarie? The letter to her was not meant as mere propaganda – it was a genuine cry from the heart of a priest who had been sickened by what he had seen in the refugee camps and desperately wanted to alert people to respond to the needs of the people there. He sent a copy of the leaflet, with its picture of Rosemarie, to her mother along with the parcel of clothing. In due course she was able to send a letter of thanks back to him. But the story did not end there.

Twenty years later, in the very different world of the 1960s, when Fr Werenfried's international work had extended to cover what was by then being called the Third

World, and its name had been alerted from *Oostpriestherhulp* ('Help for Eastern Priests') and then 'Iron Curtain Church Relief' to the more all-embracing 'Aid to the Church in Need', he met Rosemarie again. It was in India. A packed ferry-boat was jammed with people. They had to stay on one side of the vessel as the other was occupied by a jeep belonging to an orphanage. It was driven by a German nun. She worked with the poorest children, rescuing tiny girls from starvation in dustbins and gutters and giving them hope and a home. Her name was Sister Rosemarie. When she got talking to the tall Norbertine as they jumped ashore, she gasped when he said his name. She was little Rosemarie – and later at her orphanage she was able to show him the old photograph of herself and the leaflet he had written about her. As she showed him round the orphanage, she introduced him to the children. The stories were in a sense a repetition of those Fr Werenfried had met on a different continent more than two decades earlier: 'That baby was found on the beach just before the tide came in . . . That dear little boy has two little sisters here; the mother died of starvation and the father is unknown . . . That very tiny one is six years old and was found playing with the corpse of her mother who had died of starvation . . .'

When Fr Werenfried left, she gave him back the original photo (it is still kept in the archives today, and copies form part of audio-visual displays telling the story of Aid to the Church in Need). On the back she had written her thanks: the doll and the chocolate she had received in the refugee camp had been the first indications that God cared about her. She felt that she owed her own vocation as a nun to that experience, and on joining the convent had taken the name Sister Rosemarie as a private tribute to the priest who had helped her and who had given her that name in his appeal letter.

This story illustrates what was to become a hallmark of Iron Curtain Church Relief – the way in which lives became interwoven and events became bound up with one another. This was to continue again and again as the work developed and grew into the massive international charity under the name Aid to the Church in Need. It was never just an ordinary charity – it always produced extra-ordinary twists and turns, as if to emphasise that it was all somehow the work of something more than just people struggling to help one another. There was this mysterious 'other' quality to the whole enterprise, right from the start.

Nowhere was this more evident than in the story which, later, Fr Werenfried loved to tell as being central to his whole inspiration for the work in those very earliest days – the story of one particular Flemish village.

Notes

1. Extracts from the report of the Tripartite Conference of Berlin (Potsdam) 17 July–2 August 1945, section XIII, *Documents on Germany Under Occupation*, Oxford University Press, 1955.
2. Ibid., Cmnd. 6648. Statement by the Governments of the United Kingdom, the United States, the USSR, and the Provisional Government of the French Republic on zones of occupation in Germany, 5 June 1945.
3. *They call me the Bacon Priest*, Werenfried van Straaten, Haarlem, 1961.
4. *Documents on Germany Under Occupation*; Control Council plans for the transfer of the German population to be moved from Austria, Czechoslovakia, Hungary and Poland into the four occupied zones of Germany, 20 November 1945.
5. Ibid. Agreement between British and Polish representatives and the Combined Repatriation Executive, on the transfer of the German population from Poland, 14 February 1946.

Chapter Three

Fr Werenfried had coined the expression 'rucksack priests' to describe the German refugee priests who, initially in the refugee camps and then in the areas where the displaced people were settled, served them and shared their poverty and hardships.

The concept of a rucksack priest captured the imagination of Catholic people and the name stuck. At about the same time, Fr Werenfried also acquired a nickname – one that appalled his mother, who considered it most undignified for her priest son, but which was to remain with him for over fifty years. He became the 'Bacon Priest'.

Iron Curtain Church Relief had begun in an almost haphazard way – simply the collection of funds and goods from people in the area around Tongerlo, and their transportation to the refugees arriving in Germany. But gradually, as the organisation took shape, Fr Werenfried began a series of appeals, speaking and preaching at churches and Catholic parish events across Flanders.

He recalled:

After my first encounter with the distress of defeated Germany, I returned to the Abbey deeply shocked. On my arrival I found that a retreat for priests was being held. I was invited to give a conference and I spoke for an hour and a half on the subject that filled my mind and heart. At the end I went round with my hat and took my first collection for my protegees. This hat was afterwards to become famous for the millions it has collected. Some of the priests present asked me to come and preach on the subject in their parishes.

One of these invitations included a tea-party at the local women's association. This religious-minded society was celebrating its golden jubilee, and besides cakes and tarts and thick ham and cheese sandwiches, the farmers' wives felt the need of an official speaker. I was invited to enlighten the well-to-do agricultural circles on the subject of the bitter distress suffered in Germany.

I must have spoken well that afternoon. A hundred and fifty well-nourished country women forgot the fragrant coffee urns and the piles of tasty food and shed tears of pity for the hard fate of their former enemies. When my barrage on their tender country hearts was ended, there was a dead silence. Even the parish priest could not utter a word for the tears rolling down his cheeks. As nobody spoke a word I rose once more and declared encouragingly that the time had now come for the collection. The priest and the farmers' wives unanimously nodded their acquiescence, but then a better idea suddenly struck me. I proposed that each of those present should take a not-too-small piece of bacon out of the chimney and present it over the next few days at the presbytery. At the end of the week I would come with the car to collect it.

That was how the bacon campaign began, and the Bacon Priest got his name. The farmers of Flanders were famous for their bacon and in that first parish more than a ton of it was collected. It was all rushed to Tongerlo where a refrigerated room was made ready. From there it could be transported to the hungry people in the camps.

The campaign spread rapidly: 'Soon not a week passed without my speaking twice or three times at the tea parties of the country guilds. Monsignor Cruysberghs, chairman of the Farmers' League, came once to listen to my narrative and suggested that we should extend the scheme throughout the whole of Flanders. He introduced me at the regional meetings of the district heads and supported my appeal with the whole weight of his authority and rhetorical talent.

From then on began the tour through the villages and hamlets of Flanders. I took with me old Vercammen, a good friend of the Abbey. Evening after evening we returned home with eight or ten hundredweight of salted bacon and a hatful of money, until at last the poor old Peugeot sagged through the springs. Truckloads of bacon came from Flanders and Limburg and were unloaded before the astonished eyes of the Abbey visitors.

A cool storeroom was found beside the kitchen into which bacon was piled until it soon reached the ceiling. With bare feet and armed with great knives, the novices of Tongerlo struggled once a week through this mountain of bacon. They cut the bacon down to size – in those days we were allowed to send to Germany only parcels weighing not more than two pounds – and packed them into grease-proof paper, then in boxes and cases to be sent to Germany under the auspices of the Caritas Catholic organisation.

That was the beginning of the great Bacon

Campaign to which hundreds of Iron Curtain priests and thousands of children owe their good health and perhaps their lives.

It was a farmer's wife in the town of Turnhout who first called Fr Werenfried, the Bacon Priest. A Catholic newspaper picked up the name and ran it as a headline over a feature interview, and a legend had been born.

In fact the bacon campaign was only a small part of a much bigger crusade, and in any case could only be run during the winter months as it was impossible to transport the meat in the summer. A financial substitute was soon found – farmers could set aside a pig to be the 'church pig' – when slaughtered, this animal's meat would be sold and the funds go direct to Iron Curtain Church Relief.

Although his family had historically been farmers, Fr Werenfried knew nothing about agriculture or the meat trade. He learned fast. When he discovered the possibilities of importing good quality meat at a low cost from Argentina, he started negotiations for this with a meat processor who offered to turn it into sausages. For advice, Fr Werenfried turned to one of his brother monks at Tongerlo, Fr Dominic, who ran the Abbey farm. Over long talks in the cowshed and the pigsty, he learned how the best meat is produced and the pitfalls to be avoided. It meant that he was able to talk to others in the trade on their own terms.

Fr Werenfried pretended he was embarrassed by the Bacon Priest name but in fact he relished it. His crusade now had a definite identity, and the clumsy choir-monk had a cause to which he would give his heart. The name had a self-mockery that he liked: it made sense of his large frame, his sometimes cumbersome enthusiasm. He liked the idea of being identified with the pigs, and enjoyed the story of the visitor who arrived at the Abbey and asked for the Bacon Priest. 'He's in the pigsty,' he was told. 'But I've never met him before. How shall I recognise him?' 'He's the one with the biretta'.

In Germany too, where he was beginning to be known and loved as a true friend, the name stuck, and the *Speckpater* became part of people's lives, and vocabulary.

The relief effort going in to Germany was of course part of a wider scene as Europe slowly recovered from the wounds of the Second World War. Fr Werenfried's was not the only charity sending aid into Germany. But it had a unique role – it offered spiritual as well as practical aid, and helped the Catholic refugees to rally together around their priests, forming parishes and communities which helped to give them a sense of identity and to foster hope for the future.

Several years later, when the new state of West Germany – the Federal Republic of Germany – had been brought into existence and had its own government, the Federal Minister for Expellees, Dr Hans Lukashek, spoke at a conference organised by Iron Curtain Church Relief at Hilversum, Holland. It was the first Church in Need conference and was held at Drakenburgh High School under the joint chairmanship of Abbot Stalmans and a layman, J. B. G. M. Ritter de van der Schuren, chairman of the Catholic Working Party for Spiritual Renewal. In his speech, later published by the Federal Ministry, Dr Lukashek described the massive human problems that resulted from the expelling of so many millions of people from their homes and sending them to a country where so much of the housing had already been destroyed by aerial bombardment. After detailing all that had been done to cope – and outlining the problems that still existed, ranging from how to pay the pensions of those who had been officials in the old Germany, to industrial training and jobs for the young – he spoke of how charitable assistance, both from within Germany and from other nations, had made a difference:

> The help of every kind given to expellees cannot be estimated. Even the amount done by the voluntary welfare institutions can only be approximately guessed at since only certain services can be statistically confirmed ...

He mentioned the provision of shelter, clothing, meals, beds, household linen, and care for the sick:

> It is a deeply felt wish on my part to take this opportunity of thanking very heartily all organisations at home and abroad which have helped expellees to Germany. Charity does not alone consist of what is given but of how it is given, since the spirit of Christian charity is only fulfilled by 'bearing one another's burdens ...'

Throughout 1948, '49, and '50 Fr Werenfried's campaigning work flourished. Funds poured in, together with massive amounts of material aid. The Abbey at Tongerlo was in danger of being overwhelmed.

Fr Werenfried always particularly liked to recall the story of Vinkt, a town in Flanders which had suffered hugely under the German occupation. A large number of its men had been ruthlessly shot by the Germans and lay buried in the churchyard. The families were still mourning their loss. It was not a town where it was going to be easy appealing for help for German refugees. When the rumour went around that a priest was arriving who

intended to do just that, there were angry voices. And yet
... in the evening, after all the preaching was over, gifts
started to arrive, with people hurrying secretly and
privately to the presbytery to give what they could. The
parish adopted a rucksack priest. It went on to forge deep
and lasting bonds with German refugee families. This, for
Fr Werenfried, showed the genuine triumph of the
Christian message – that love is stronger than hate, that
forgiveness and kindliness is possible and achievable.

The Catholic women of Flanders were urged to donate
any clothes they could to Iron Curtain Church Relief for
despatch to Germany. Parish halls were used as collection
points, and from there trucks and lorries brought the goods
to Tongerlo. Relays of volunteers then sorted and stacked
the clothes and shoes, which were packed into bales and
then sent off in trucks to Germany – fifteen tons of clothing
at a time. Meanwhile the priests among the refugees had
been gathering lists from their people as to what was needed
– cards with shoe sizes and specific requirements were
processed and the goods were gradually delivered to their
destinations. Parcels of clothing went into cellars, attics
and bunkers where the refugees were housed.

Fr Werenfried later recalled:

Immediately, the wave of gratitude flowed back to the
West. The first letters arriving in Tongerlo were like
the intonation of a paeon of joy resounding in
growing and mighty harmony over the towns and
villages and cottages of this small country, a country
that, too, had suffered much in the course of the
centuries, but one where hearts had remained warm
and generous – a lovable country.

This Flemish land was not of course able to reverse
the decree of Potsdam with its aftermath of injustice

and sorrow. But the energetic love of these good people did succeed in keeping 3,000 itinerant priests alive, and in supporting and aiding them in such a way that they could help others ...

Some forms of aid were uniquely Catholic, filling corners that no one else might have noticed. For the Catholic refugees from Silesia and East Prussia, now mostly living in Protestant areas of Germany, the celebration of Catholic feasts and ceremonies was of enormous importance. Their priests tried to find places where Mass could be celebrated, but it was hard. Sometimes, a local Protestant church was available through the kindness of its pastor. Sometimes, a room could be rented. In camps, some services could be held out of doors.

For children's First Holy Communion, the traditional white dresses seemed only an impossible dream. But Fr Werenfried responded positively when he heard of the sacrifices that people were prepared to make to try to get something special for their children to wear. What a difference it would make if First Holy Communion could be celebrated with joy in traditional style, even amid the misery of refugee life! An appeal went out across Holland and Belgium for white dresses that might be tucked away in attics and cupboards – and the result was a staggering ten thousand dresses, some unearthed by mothers who had hunted out something kept for years, others donated by children who had recently worn them for their own ceremonies and had wanted to keep them to cherish or to wear in further processions, but had chosen to forfeit this so that a refugee child could have a chance to dress beautifully for one special day ...

Then came the sweets campaign. Children were asked to give up their sweets during Lent, and to send them in to

36

Iron Curtain Church Relief. With them came notes and letters, sometimes from the children themselves, sometimes from adults who wanted to record moving anecdotes and examples of children's heroism in giving up sweets and treats they had really wanted, in order to give joy to refugee children they would never meet. A total of sixty tons of chocolates, caramels, peppermints, biscuits, peardrops, toffees and other delights was collected. No sweets were wasted. All were carefully packed into little paper parcels and tied with attractive ribbons to be taken to Germany where they were distributed to children who hadn't seen sweets for years.

The key to it all was that the gifts were personal. The child who was determined to give up her largest and most cherished chocolate egg – holding back tears as she insistently handed it to the nun who was collecting sweets at the parish hall. The little girl who gave up her place as an angel in the parish procession so that her beautiful white First Communion dress could be passed on to a refugee child. The little boy who, after hearing Fr Werenfried preach, wandered for hours the next day with his moneybox and a warm bar of chocolate in his hands, looking for the Bacon Priest so that he could hand over these precious gifts. The woman whose husband died in a German concentration camp but who now quietly handed over his suit to go to a German in need … This sort of love has a quality of heroism that is beyond price.

When the letters of thanks came back, Fr Werenfried would quote from them in sermons and appeals. Even the names of the refugee children rang oddly in Western ears – Kalwe and Sulew, Stoya, Lothar, Edeltraut, Merija, Erika, Tatjana, Teresza. These were children who were writing from camps or temporary accommodation, who had often lost father or mother or both, who had little prospect of proper education or of a place they could truly call 'home'. A packet of sweets from a Flemish address, sent with the love of children who had made real sacrifices to ensure the gift, meant a great deal.

Nor was it only the people of Flanders who were giving. Within Germany itself, those who had something to give were doing so generously, as were people in Austria. In Switzerland, generous gifts were collected – in one town a young man chased after Fr Werenfried's truck as it was leaving, and threw in a heavy envelope. It turned out to contain ten thousand Swiss francs – a gift from a young man who was about to be married and had been given the money by a family trust. He and his fiancée believed that it could be better used by the Bacon Priest and they gladly gave it away to him. People donated rings and necklaces, gold coins they had saved in case hard times came, savings that had been put aside for special holiday trips. People gave Fr Werenfried money in odd envelopes or battered purses. Sometimes there would be letters attached, begging for prayers or explaining some personal story.

'He would come back from his preaching', his assistant, Germaine van de Roy, recalls. 'He had big pockets; one pocket would be filled with money, the other one with letters. And he'd put everything on the table and he'd say – here you are, you sort it out.'

And still the work expanded. The rucksack priests must be brought together, a strategy worked out, realistic plans made for the future. Could cars be provided for them? Churches for their dispersed flocks? What about the refugees who were in the Eastern Zone of Germany, where the Communist authorities were leaning heavily on all signs of Church life? What about further afield? That was how the Konigstein gatherings began.

Chapter Four

The work of Iron Curtain Church Relief was, in these early days, very much a Flanders activity, centred on the Abbey at Tongerlo. It was here that all the aid was collected, with clothes being stacked up and bacon stored. It was to here that Fr Werenfried returned after his preaching trips or visits to Germany, with his pockets full of money or of notes listing things that needed to be done, people needing specific help.

But increasingly, there was action within Germany, especially as the priests from the eastern territories began to gather together for mutual support and help.

A seminary for young men training for the priesthood was being established at Konigstein, about fifteen miles outside Frankfurt, a beautiful town surrounded by hills and dominated by the rather romantic ruin of a castle standing on top of one of them, overlooking the cobbled streets and old-fashioned houses and shops. Unlike so many similar towns and villages across Germany, this one had not been bombed in the massive Allied air raids. Its little parish church still stood with its beautiful baroque interior. A statue of the Grand Duke of Luxembourg – whose family had owned a country house in the town and were frequent visitors there – stood in an attractive park. There were bakers' shops and old-fashioned coffee-shops along the main street where, when prosperous times came again, ladies could meet to chat.

On the outskirts of the town stood a former barracks, originally built to house French troops at the end of the First World War. Now it was to be given over to the displaced priests of Germany's former eastern territories. An extraordinary collection of young men started to gather there.

Fr Werenfried was later to recall:

What brave, generous men were those first seminarians! After the catastrophe, they heard God singing in their hearts and recklessly followed Him. They had lost their homes, and their families were scattered like feathers before the wind. Driven away from their villages and towns they had experienced all the hardships of racial migration. They were turned from homelands where their ancestors had lived for centuries, some from the German language enclaves of Bukowina, some from remote Bessarabia, from Batchka, from Rumania or Bulgaria, or the steppes of Hungary, from Silesia, Ermland, Pommerania or Sudeten. Some may have survived the death-march from East Prussia or perhaps passed through the bloody Stations of the Cross in the Polish and Czech camps, but most had returned from the bitter years of captivity as prisoners of war, without a chance of seeing their lost homes again and without knowing what had become of their families. Forlorn young men among the sixteen million that had gone under in the storm of Potsdam.

Many of these young men wore scraps of old German uniforms – they had no other clothes. The former barracks had very basic facilities. There had been a German field hospital in the premises in the last days of the war, and the seminarians were able to use their beds and sheets. Food was very short – as everywhere in Germany. As the refugee exile community began to gather at Konigstein, they organised themselves: a small group of nuns from East Prussia took over the catering arrangements for the seminary, and an assorted group of exiled German professors became the basis of the teaching staff.

Fr Werenfried recalled:

There was also a junior seminary. In the first class there were then forty-five children from age twelve to fifteen. The fathers of fourteen of them had died in battle or had been reported missing. The fathers of eleven others had been deported to Siberia. Seven of them told me that their mothers had been carried off by the Russians. Two of them had seen their mothers die of exhaustion along the road to exile. Nineteen had no contact whatsoever with their families. Forty-five children with forty-five different tragedies.

To Konigstein had come not only men who sought to become priests, but exiled bishops who needed men to tend their scattered flocks. Bishop Maximillian Kaller was Bishop of Ermland, in territory that was now to become part of Poland. The agreements of Yalta and Potsdam, which drew a new map for Europe, were written by the victors of the war and thus the effective powers in Europe. The Vatican had little choice but to go along with them. The Polish people who would be settled in the area where formerly German-speaking people had lived would need bishops of their own. Bishop Kaller found himself not only an exile but the leader of a drifting group of people who had no diocese where they felt at home, and a confused sense of identity in the Church. Poland's Bishop Augustine Hlond was now bishop of the diocese where Bishop Kaller had once presided.

Bishop Adolphus Kinderman was another leader among the exiled Germans. A former professor of theology at Prague University, and director of a major seminary, he was detained in a Czech concentration camp before being finally exiled to West Germany. Settling in Konigstein, he and his small team of helpers had become a rallying-point for refugees seeking lost members of their families, a distribution point for aid – the basement was filled with clothing and other goods for the desperately needy exiles – and a focal point for all the exiled priests. He established the seminary at Konigstein and gathered support for his exiled people – and he found a natural ally and supporter in Fr Werenfried. Bishop Kinderman was a speaker at the Church in Need congresses which began to be an annual event associated with Iron Curtain Church Relief. It was he who had talked, in the very first days of the expulsions, to the Abbot-General of the Norbertine order, begging for help for his people. At Konigstein he now organised the exiled German priests who were scattered across West Germany. The exiles had been settled mostly in the Protestant districts where they found little or no local infrastructure to give them assistance. He begged Fr Werenfried for help as these priests were stretched beyond the limits of their strength.

Many of the rucksack priests went from place to place on foot or with a battered bicycle, celebrating Mass for their communities in all the odd places where the refugees had been settled. Sometimes this meant four or five Masses, all in barns or attics or rented rooms, and never with adequate nourishment in-between the long journeys. Over three centuries earlier, at the Reformation,

Germany had effectively been divided into Protestant and Catholic districts. In some of the wide-ranging Protestant areas, there had been little if any Catholic presence in the intervening years. German Catholics tended to refer to these districts as the 'diaspora'. It was extremely hard for the exiled Catholics from places such as Silesia with a strong Catholic tradition, who were now suddenly living in places where there was no Catholic church within miles, and no sense of home. They had been used to crowded village churches, a whole Catholic culture, great celebrations on feast-days. They had a sense of loneliness and bewilderment at being in what was, for them, a bleak and alien culture where their religion was deemed strange. It took massive efforts by priests, travelling from one isolated group to another, to foster a sense of community and to renew links and create an atmosphere of hope. Several rucksack priests died from heart failure brought on by sheer exhaustion in these districts in the first years after the war.

At Konigstein, the seminarians were trained, and the rucksack priests came for rest and refreshment. The priests received the basic help they needed: a spare shirt, decent shoes, writing materials. They arrived wearing ill-assorted scraps of ragged clothing, and carrying few if any possessions. Many arrived limping or struggling with sticks as they had been wounded in the war. Many, like the young seminarians and the lay people they were serving, had lost all links with their families.

For such men, the aid that came from Catholic families in Flanders was doubly precious. It represented not only things they badly needed – clothes, books, shoes – but also love and care, a recognition that they were not pariahs and that they had a right to be priests and to serve the Catholic exiled Germans who had been caught up in the aftermath of a massive war and now faced years of hard-ship.

All the aid in those early years was personal. Families and parishes in Flanders adopted, through Iron Curtain Church Relief, an exiled priest. They wrote him letters and sent him parcels. Children wrote to him with assur-ances of their prayers. Catholic schools got involved – a class would adopt a priest and would hold meetings to plan what sweets, gifts, and necessities they would put in his next parcel. After one of Fr Werenfried's preaching trips around Flanders, gifts would pour in to Tongerlo – often with letters attached. Families shared their own sorrow of war and expressed a longing for friendship and reconciliation.

With all this came criticism – the first sparks of what was to be a continuous barrage. Fr Werenfried was accused of running a pan-Germanic organisation with Nazi lean-ings, of pandering to Flemish pro-German sentiment. There were tensions here. Some Flemish people had undoubtedly supported the Germans in the war, and some young men had even volunteered to fight with the German Army on the Eastern Front, seeing this as part of a big international crusade against Communist Russia. But Iron Curtain Church Relief had no political or racial ideology and was not involved with any of this: it existed simply and solely to help the poor and struggling exiled catholics from the East and to do what it could to safe-guard the future of the Church in a Europe hideously battered by war. Its message was always one of peace and reconciliation.

The exiled Germans from the East were now being joined by large numbers who were fleeing voluntarily, hurrying to leave the territories now ruled by Communist governments. Camps in West Germany were set up to receive them, but it was extremely difficult to keep up with the flow. Some were given money and food and told to return: there simply was no room for them. But people continued to flee from East to West. The Russian zone of Germany was about to become the 'German Democratic Republic', a 'Workers and Farmers State', dominated entirely by Russia and with a completely Communist Government. People fled as the reality of this became only too apparent. In the Western Zones of Germany, preparations were being made for the establishment of a genuinely democratic nation-state, the Federal Republic of Germany. As the 1940s ended and the 1950s began, there were two Germanies – and eventually they would be divided by a hideous barrier, with barbed wire and machine-guns set up by the Communist East Germany preventing people fleeing from East to West. Those who had fled in those early years counted themselves fortunate to be on the western side.

During the late 1940s the pattern of Fr Werenfried's life – in so far as it could be said to have any pattern – consisted of preaching tours around Flanders interspersed with trips to Germany. These last included visits to Konigstein and many trips to camps and to exiled communities. After such visits, he would write impassioned begging letters asking for help which went to churches and Catholic schools in Belgium and Holland.

Among the refugees, there were many bitter stories. Young men, in particular, felt that the future held no hope. There seemed no chance of a job, a challenge, the chance to create a new life and a new home. In his visits to the groups of exiled Germans, Fr Werenfried spent much of his time not only distributing material aid, but listening to personal stories and trying to offer encouragement and solace and hope.

The Allied governments who had charge of the three Western zones of Germany were presiding over a region which, although desperately poor and with its major cities in ruins, carried the seeds of renewal. The German reputation for hard work – both feared and respected throughout the rest of Europe – teamed up with the Allied commitment to a prosperous and free Germany in the heart of Europe, economically bound to its neighbours and unable to wage war on them. Programmes of rebuilding cities took shape. The young trainees for the priesthood at Konigstein spent their summers working at these, and the autumn and spring terms studying theology and other subjects in preparation for ordination.

Back in Flanders, the work of Iron Curtain Church Relief had become almost an established part of life in many parishes. The letters that flowed back from the exiled Germans became part of Catholic community life. German children had started to write letters in response to the sweets campaign. Thousands of German refugee children had received a little ribboned package with a note inside saying 'At the request of Iron Curtain Church Relief a child in Flanders saved these sweets instead of eating them, so that it could bring you a little happiness. Will you write a note back? Here is the address ...'

As the work expanded, plans were made for some of the German children to have holidays in Flanders, where they could enjoy fresh air and good food with country families. The first batch of German children arrived in 1950. A new decade was beginning. For Iron Curtain Church Relief the work among refugees, although still very important, would gradually give way to fresh initiative among Poles, Czechs, Slovaks, and others, in the nations behind the Iron Curtain where the Church was struggling to survive.

Chapter Five

At Tongerlo, Fr Werenfried was still very much a member of the community, albeit one who seemed to come and go virtually at will. It was here, and in rented rooms in a nearby town, that the goods were stored for onward despatch to Germany. The whole community of the Abbey at Tongerlo was involved, to some degree, in those first years, in the work of Aid to the Church in Need.

In his earlier years in the community, Fr Werenfried had had time for calligraphy – he created beautiful lettering for some of the books used for prayers and hymns in the choir, and these can still be seen there. He was a scholar in Latin and in Greek. But now he seemed mostly to live on the road, hurrying back to the Abbey often late at night and unexpectedly.

A member of the community during these years was Fr Patrick Gallagher, an Englishman who would later become prior of the Norbertine community at Corpus Christi church in Manchester.

'Werenfried had the reputation of being a practical joker,' he said. 'One night one of his friends decided to get his own back on him. Knowing that Werenfried would arrive back extremely late, in the silence and darkness of the Abbey, he stacked up huge quantities of kitchenware – saucepans and casseroles and big tin dishes – behind a door and there was the most magnificent crash when Werenfried strode in ...'

The press had now established the character of the *Speckpater*, the Bacon Priest, as a well-known figure in Catholic life in Belgium, in Holland, Austria, and Germany. As West German economic fortunes became better with the establishment of the new Deutschmark currency, and the creation of the Federal Republic, Fr Werenfried was able to do something that at one time would have seemed unimaginable – preaching within Germany itself and collecting money there for poorer people elsewhere.

In May 1951 he was featured in a Catholic paper for German miners, called 'After the shift' (ie to read when relaxing after working hours), which carried the slogan 'Europe – the way of love'. It told the story of how the people in Flanders who had suffered in the war were sending aid to Germany, repeating the tale of the village where relatives of those who had been shot by the Germans were among the first to give. The paper described Fr Werenfried as a country boy from Flanders who was now 'a new apostle of our time'. It quoted an elderly priest enthusing about Werenfried's charisma and reported that in September the Bacon Priest would be preaching in Speyer.

In 1953 Fr Werenfried preached in a car park in Munich, in the heart of one of the most Catholic parts of Germany. The press reported that people had travelled from every part of Bavaria to hear the *Speckpater*.

In 1954 the Munchener Katholische Kirchenzeitung printed a picture of him addressing a crowd of 3,000 in Munich and noted that after visiting the city he was off on a tour of Bavaria and then to Ghent in Belgium.

In 1950 he initiated the 'chapel trucks', special lorries

which opened up at the side to reveal an altar, with the doors acting as side panels and depicting religious scenes. Such a truck, carrying clothes and gifts for the refugee Germans in the exile communities, could also act as a temporary church. Mass was celebrated at the altar and crowds gathered. The money for these trucks came from Flanders, and the vehicles were blessed in a massive ceremony at Konigstein.

Under the slogan 'Vehicles for God', Fr Werenfried also obtained hundreds of small cars for use by the rucksack priests. These too were blessed in big ceremonies where they were decorated with green branches, and hymns and prayers were sung in both Flemish and German and people from the donor nations of Belgium and Holland met and prayed with the German priests and lay people.

The chapel trucks covered hundreds of miles across Germany taking gifts and spiritual relief to the exiles. They were so arranged that the driver and the priest could sleep and eat inside if necessary, and they could carry large amounts of material aid. Their arrival among the refugees was a sign for a bustle of activity. Sometimes a canopy would be clipped to the side to accommodate people for Mass, creating a large temporary church. There were always gifts to be distributed, sermons preached, and a message of hope and encouragement given.

The chapel trucks returned regularly to Konigstein for repairs and renovations. The Dutch and Belgian people who had provided them were proud of these vehicles, and stories about the chapel trucks, their drivers and the communities they served, appeared regularly in the Catholic press.

1953 saw the foundation of something very close to Fr Werenfried's heart – a new and unique religious movement, to be called the 'Building Companions'. These young men were committed to working at building homes for refugees and churches for their needs. It was a bold and imaginative gesture, a response to the crying need for housing. Thousands and thousands of families in Germany and in Austria were still living in camps or in various forms of temporary accommodation. It was impossible to preach to them about the virtues of Christian family life when they were forced to live in cramped and often sordid conditions, with little or no privacy.

'The idea of a building fraternity arose from a meeting I had with a little refugee girl in a hutment camp,' Fr Werenfried later recalled. 'I gave the child a picture and said she must hang this up on the wall at home. "We have no wall, Father!" she said. They had no wall! They lived somewhere in the middle of a hut, without walls, without protection against the awareness of life, day and night!'

Fr Werenfried later paid tribute to two men who helped to establish the Building Companions – a Colonel van Coppenolle who carried out the preparatory research which involved trips to Germany and careful tactful work to establish whether volunteer labour from Holland and Belgium could be used in this way, and Fritz Kroger, who was the manager of a Christian trade union in Germany for building labourers. There was much opposition to the whole scheme initially, but it was finally brought to fruition and the Companions were established and began work on a number of major projects.

The main work was the creation of houses for refugees. The Building Companions lived and worked as a community, with prayer in common at the beginning and end of each day, and plenty of hard work in-between. They were idealistic volunteers, and cynics believed that teams made up of such young men would be unequal to the task of creating solid houses in bleak areas of muddy territory. But the cynics were confounded. One of the first projects involved giving assistance with a self-help scheme for refugees that had been launched in one district, where refugees were housed in a camp and went out every day to dig and build. The problem was that while the fitter men among the refugee families could do this work, there were many who were disabled who could not manage the heavier tasks. There were also many young mothers who were widows, and many old people – so there were many families who were unlikely to see their homes completed. The Building Companions set to work with a will, and the whole venture was completed a year ahead of schedule.

All this was deeply satisfying, and it drove Fr Werenfried on to make bigger promises. In Innsbruck in Austria in 1954 he announced that he was investing 60,000 schillings in a settlement project. In two years of building work, 120 families – some 600–700 people – had been given new homes. But housing remained the greatest single need in Europe.

'He was very enthusiastic about his work,' Germaine van de Roy recalled. 'One had the impression he wanted to save the whole world. And he didn't think how much this would cost. He said for instance "We need to send care packages to Berlin. I've visited a camp there – the needs are enormous." So he ordered care packages, not knowing how he would pay for them, but trusting he would find a solution. He wrote letters to his benefactors, he went preaching. He always succeeded – right from the very beginning. It was his word, written or spoken, that made people open their purses and give him all their money – in fact, even more than they could really afford.'

With the Building Companions flourishing, and with preaching tours that now included Germany, the image of the Bacon Priest had turned into a sort of legend. The

German newspapers *Der Spiegel* in April 1954 described him as the 'Master of collection' under a picture showing him with his hat, already battered and destined to become much more so, as it was used for hundreds of church collections over the years. And the Archbishop of Cologne, Cardinal Frings said that Fr Werenfried was 'a new Genghis Khan' because he swept everything bare wherever he went! People relished the notion that this priest could stir people up to give away so much, and collect staggering sums of money that could be used for the poor and needy. It was a strong and vibrant image that, in itself, projected a message of hope and of a positive future. Perhaps it was this, as much as the money itself, that the German exiles and the people behind the Iron Curtain really needed.

The work behind the Iron Curtain happened, of necessity, with great secrecy. In those very earliest days, when Stalin's hand still gripped Eastern Europe, the plight of the Church there was dark indeed. Many bishops and priests were imprisoned. There were show trials and appalling things done in secret rooms in prisons. The Church in the West was powerless to do anything. It was hard to get news of what was really taking place. Official radio stations of Communist nations gave out only propaganda.

The annual Church in Need conferences in Konigstein from 1952 onwards brought together people from various Eastern European countries and many senior clergy and laity from the Church in the West. In September 1952 the conference heard talks on 'The Communist struggle against the Church' by a Jesuit, Fr de Vries, based in Rome, with a follow-up discussion on 'What is the Church waiting for from us?' and details of the latest projects from Fr Werenfried. In 1955 Mgr Kinderman was among the speakers with the title 'Bolshevism's struggle against the Church' and topics from other speakers included 'The way of Lenin and Stalin' and 'Bolshevism as an ersatz religion'. But the most moving speakers came from behind the Iron Curtain.

'A Hungarian dignitary, a Polish Monsignor, a bearded Russian priest and a fiery Ukrainian gave evidence with quiet sadness, or passionately, according to their nature, of the imprisoned shepherds and beaten flocks of their country. Accurately and with moving piety they made long lists of bloody sacrifices that mounted up to a sum total of bitterness and glory. The situation in the no-man's land between East and West, the Soviet zones of Germany and Austria and the desolate areas along the front of the Universal Church, was once more surveyed. The bloodshed and lamentations of Albania and the Baltic states were heart-rending. A bishop driven out of China closed the sombre line of witnesses.'

Fr Werenfried went on to recall:

This [1952] congress was a turning point in our work. After this, ICCR altered its course. With the German 'economic miracle' in sight, we thenceforward gave precedence in our relief action to the non-German groups of displaced persons above those Germans driven from their homes abroad, whose problems were slowly but surely nearing their solution. Here we took a leap over the Iron Curtain and decided definitely to devote a part of our energies to the preparation of a better future for Eastern Europe.'

It is difficult for a later generation, witnesses to the collapse of Communism across Europe, to grasp fully just what a threat it posed in the 1950s. The Soviet Union,

Communist since 1917 and already with huge numbers of martyrs within her borders, had now gained control over all of Eastern Europe. Communism was an ideology which insisted on a completely new idea of human beings and their reason for existence. All private property was, in theory, banned and provision for everything from housing to agriculture was the preserve of the State. Religion, as representing an area of life where the State could not intervene – in the mind and the soul – posed a threat and challenge. Christianity and the Church were associated with all the centuries and eras that had gone before – tangible evidence that man had created homes and schools, universities, farms, art, science, hospitals and great feats of engineering without the notion of Communism. This reminder of the past, and its sense of bonding with the generations that had gone before, must be crushed.

The early post-war years in Eastern Europe saw the show trials of several Catholic leaders. Cardinal Stepinac in Croatia, Yugoslavia, was sentenced to years in prison for alleged collaboration with the Nazis. There was no evidence that he had ever collaborated in such a way. But he died under imprisonment. In Hungary, Cardinal Mindszenty was arraigned in a grisly show trial after beatings and torture and imprisoned. In Poland Cardinal Wyzsinksi of Warsaw was taken away under house arrest and kept in a remote district where he could not communicate with his priests or people.

Everywhere, the Church was stripped of its property, banned from using its own buildings including monasteries and schools, hounded from its place in community life, denounced in the media with repeated allegations of sordid crimes. It became impossible for members of religious communities to live together, and extremely

difficult for a bishop to train young men for the priesthood. Children were subjected to massive anti-religious
indoctrination in schools and chivvied into Communist
youth organisations. And, because the Communist
economic system meant the theft of all the means of
production, and the stifling of creative work and initia-
tives, there was poverty, poor nourishment, bad housing,
inefficient transport, making everyday life extremely difficult and the struggle to maintain religious practice hard.

For anyone who tried to speak out in support of the
Church or in opposition to the new regime, the horrors
of prison, or the labour camps of the Soviet Union, were
waiting. These were the years of torture and beatings, of
trains trundling starving prisoners northward to the
camps beyond the Arctic Circle. In Latvia and Lithuania,
thousands of people were simply rounded up and
deported in this way, dying of hunger and thirst in the
transit trains, or worked to exhaustion as slaves in the
camps. Poland, which had experienced a Soviet incursion
in September 1939 when the Soviets arrived from the
East just days after Germany had invaded from the West,
had already lost many of her people. Polish Army officers, arrested by the Soviets, had been shot in Katyn
Forest. Families in eastern Poland had been hounded out
of their homes and sent eastwards to the Soviet Union,
never to be seen again.

Although a barrier divided Communist and non-
Communist Europe – and was enforced with guns and
barbed wire to prevent people from escaping from East to
West – there was still a postal service, and there was a
certain amount of trade. It was possible to send in aid and
help, partly through individual packages sent in as gifts.
And, as events developed in Eastern and central Europe,
with uprisings against Communism in Berlin, in Poland,

and later most dramatically in Hungary, aid from Iron Curtain Church Relief poured in while the chinks in the curtain were opened, however briefly.

Obviously, the aid – including individual gift packages – would not travel openly under the name Iron Curtain Church Relief. On the contrary. Attempts to send parcels from Tongerlo or from any well-known address were doomed to failure. Sometimes, parcels were in any case returned, or the contents stolen by the Communist authorities. But some gifts did get through. The recipients benefited from the comfort these brought – and they were tangible evidence that people in the West knew of their plight. Staff at ICCR in Tongerlo poured over the details of postal and trade agreements between East and West, and learned how to send packages that would not fall foul of the authorities. Aid thus reached beleaguered priests, dispersed religious communities, bishops who had begun to despair and to fear that the wider Church was ignoring them.

The phrase used to describe the persecuted Church at this time was 'the Church of Silence'. With strong leadership from Rome, where Pope Pius XII took a firm line against Communism, the faithful were encouraged to pray for the conversion of Russia, and for individual Communists and for the strengthening and survival of the Church in Eastern Europe. In the western Catholic press, and in Catholic schools and organisations, figures such as Cardinals Stepinac and Mindszenty were heroes. Catholic schools and institutions were named after them in America. Funds for ICCR in Europe were collected through newsletters and rallies where information about the plight of persecuted religious leaders was given and prayers were also sought.

In a most important sense, ICCR became one of the

chief sources of news and information about the persecuted Church. Through information given by refugees,
through its letters and secret visits, through its numerous
contacts both with bishops and with various groups of
faithful Catholics, the organisation was constantly building a picture of the plight of the Church within the
countries under Communist rule. In particular, ICCR was
able to show up the front organisations created by the
Communists, such as the bogus 'Pacem in Terris' organisation for priests which purported to show that the clergy
were happy to work with and for the Communist state in
pursuit of social goals. This movement gained supporters,
because the clergy who were members were given jobs
funded by the State. But there was no real support among
the faithful, who tended to shun the pastoral ministra-
tions of such priests and to support those who took the
option of remaining loyal to Rome (which had denounced
the movement) and of upholding traditional Catholic
beliefs, traditions, and teachings.

Fr Werenfried did not launch ICCR as a major international relief or intelligence-gathering organisation. The
growth of the work happened almost by accident – a
natural progression from aid to refugees to aid across the
Iron Curtain border, always with the common aim of
trying to keep alive the Church in a divided Europe
menaced by the aftermath of war and the growth of anti-
Christian ideologies. Always, the essential aim was the
good of the Church and the survival and spread of
Christianity – expressed in tangible terms through practical gifts of food, clothing – and, increasingly – building
materials, cars, electrical equipment, books, paper – for
the human beings who were at the forefront of a persecuted and beleaguered Catholicism.

Chapter Six

In Cologne, in 1950, Fr Werenfried had collected a staggering 275,000 Deutschmarks, together with 17lbs of jewellery. Over forty people also donated their motorcycles for Iron Curtain Church Relief. All this in a city which had been reduced to ruins by Allied bombing raids only a few years earlier and where most families were living in hardship and poverty. People were living in basements or in temporary shelters, with a few pieces of rescued furniture and household goods. In response to his appeals for help for refugees, they gave him their last family heirlooms, or their only means of transport. They responded to his message that the only alternative to helping the exiled eastern refugees was chaos. A bitter, hungry, homeless people with no hope represented a threat to the whole future of Europe. The only victors would be the Communists who had gathered all of Eastern Europe into their possession and were hungry for Germany too.

In 1954 the newly created state of West Germany, by now well on the way to prosperity, presented the Bacon Priest with a special award, the Order of the Federal Republic of Germany, to thank him for the help he had given in Germany's grimmest hour.

Now ICCR looked eastward, towards the persecuted Church and its desperate needs. In February 1949 the

Hungarian State radio had broadcast the broken stammering voice of Cardinal Mindszenty, primate of Budapest and head of the Hungarian Catholic Church, answering 'igenis, igenis' – 'yes, yes it is true' at his show trial. He had been mercilessly tortured, beaten, deprived of sleep, and pitilessly interrogated until his voice and his mind were no longer his own. Like many other victims of Communism, he had come to know the horror of blood-stained walls in prison rooms, the screams of fellow victims in the night, questioning hour after hour by relays of interrogators, exhaustion, thirst, and terror.

In 1956 the Hungarian people rose up against their Communist oppressors in an electrifying and dramatic bid for freedom. The news broke across Europe on 26 October, a Friday evening. Young people had taken to the streets of Budapest, defying the authorities, ripping Communist hammer-and-sickle emblems from buildings and tearing the hated Soviet star from the centre of their national flag. They had opened the borders of their country to the West, had commandeered vehicles in the streets of their capital city and were defying soldiers and police. Fighting had broken out. Flickering television pictures in black and white began to carry the news to the West, and the cries and songs of the young freedom fighters were heard on the radio waves.

Fr Werenfried was at Tongerlo, and on hearing the news on the radio immediately rushed to the town of Louvain where he met with Father Laszlo Varga, adviser for the Hungarian work of ICCR. They by now had heard of fighting in the streets, and wounded people arriving at the frontier between Hungary and Austria. They took action immediately. By the Saturday evening a plane had already left Belgium with medical supplies, some from the Red Cross and some from Iron Curtain Church Relief.

Was this the great moment when Communism would crack? The West watched. Through the night, in Brussels, in rain outside the Hungarian Legation, Fr Werenfried and a band of followers knelt and prayed. They went on to pray outside the Russian embassy. It was the prelude to a feverish time of activity. At Tongerlo the offices were transformed into a medical dispensary and all through Saturday volunteers started to collect and prepare medicines ready for immediate despatch to Hungary. Across Flanders, ICCR supporters were also collecting medicines in church halls and in schools. The response to appeals for help was extraordinary – some hospitals donated almost the whole of their supplies. People stayed up all night packing and preparing goods, or going from house to house to ask for medicines and bandages. It became known that the Hungarian border was now open. Trucks could drive across.

At Tongerlo transport was soon ready. Trucks were filled with anything that people might need following the loss of their homes during the fighting. It was autumn and the winter was coming – stacks of clothing and shoes were packed in. ICCR help was also flowing to Hungary from Switzerland. In city after city, Catholic volunteers were collecting goods, obtaining transport, organising prayer campaigns.

On the Tuesday morning Fr Werenfried flew to Vienna, from where he would drive to Budapest. With every hour, the news from Hungary grew more thrilling. One of the first things that the young freedom fighters wanted to do was to free Cardinal Mindszenty – not only their Cardinal but also, in the absence of a king (the country had been technically a monarchy until the Second World War) their symbol of nationhood.

For Fr Werenfried, the meeting with Cardinal

Mindszenty in Budapest was a defining moment – an experience to which he would return again and again in memory in the years to come, a central and dramatic pivotal point for all that ICCR represented.

A consultation is held in Vienna with our local collaborators and with other organisations. There is hesitation and a desire to wait awhile. I decide to start immediately. I have no valid passport or visa, only my rosary. I pray the rosary with my Austrian and Hungarian friends from Vienna to Budapest. The adventure is successful. Three hours after his liberation I was to stand, with the chairman of the Austrian Caritas and a few others, in a small room with Cardinal Mindszenty. We were the first priests from the West to see him. The revolution was still going on.

It was All Saints Day. Fighting was heard on the streets, and national flags were flying from many houses. There could be no doubt that this was a genuine national revolt. The mood among some of the young freedom fighters were euphoric. Children were riding gleefully on the top of commandeered military vehicles. Soviet troops were being hounded out of the city.

But how long could this last? The faces under the big helmets, grabbed from the Army, were exhausted and grubby. Many homes in the city centre were flying black flags from their windows as a sign of mourning, as a son or husband had been killed in the fighting.

As Fr Werenfried and his colleagues talked to the Cardinal, others too were thronging to see him. People who had themselves been newly released from prison, including priests and two other bishops were among the crowd. Eagerly, they begged for news of how the West was responding to their plight, and pleaded for desperately needed help. Fr Werenfried just as eagerly scribbled down their names and addresses, promising aid parcels. Meanwhile the Cardinal, having listened to all that was going on, and talked at length to Mgr Pfeffer of the Austrian Caritas organisation, sat down to write a letter to the Catholic bishops of the world. In it, he begged for help and prayers and sent brotherly greetings from a liberated city. He entrusted this letter to Fr Werenfried for publication and as he did so he took the priest's two hands in his with a dramatic gesture: 'Father, when you return to the West, tell your friends that they are not to forget us. Ask them to pray, to keep on praying. For there is a heavy struggle ahead of us.'

It was perhaps as well that the Cardinal did not know just how heavy that struggle would be for him personally. That night, in a city where over 20,000 had already died in the fighting, and where candles were burning at makeshift memorial shrines, the small team from the West set about translating the letter and sending it out to the world. Over the next days, ICCR, back in the West, prepared aid on a massive scale: not only food and clothing and medicines but thousands and thousands of Catholic catechisms in Hungarian, together with Prayer Books and Bibles, for a Church which had been denied freedom to print anything for years. These were rushed across the border, to form the basis of the new era of freedom for the Hungarian Church, rebuilding after the ravages of Communism.

It was not to be. Although much of the aid sent by ICCR – and on a massive scale by other relief organisations of every kind – did reach people in Hungary, it was only as a tiny consolation as the great might of the Red

Army was turned upon the country and the idealistic revolt was pitilessly crushed by massive Soviet power. While Fr Werenfried, with the Belgian national radio placed at his disposal during the days of the crisis, broadcast appeals for prayer and for a spirit of solidarity with the Hungarians, the grim reality of military might rolled forward in Budapest. The West seemed powerless to help, and in any case was distracted by another event: the Suez Crisis and the threat it posed. Young idealistic Catholics across America and Western Europe had been attending rallies and volunteering to go and fight alongside the Hungarians. But to oppose the Red Army required more than mere courage. In any case, the West chose not to act. Communist power, in its grim reality of tanks and guns, rolled back over Hungary. Thousands of refugees fled to the borders and spilled over into Western Europe. Among them were some of the people that Fr Werenfried had met in Budapest and to whom he had hoped to send parcels of aid to build up a new and free country.

Cardinal Mindszenty fled, in a dramatic move in the last days of the Uprising, to the American Legation, where he would live for two decades as a symbol of his country's struggle for freedom. The bond that he had forged with Fr Werenfried was never to be broken and, as we will see, was to prove crucial to him as events developed towards the end of his life.

In the end, as far as Fr Werenfried's work was concerned, the Hungarian Uprising became a sort of icon of all that was tragic about Eastern Europe. Images of Cardinal Mindszenty appeared regularly in ICCR publications, and he was frequently invoked in Werenfried's speeches. Aid now poured into Eastern Europe on a massive and unremitting scale.

At Tongerlo, staff scrutinised every aspect of the trade

and postal regulations of every nation in the Communist bloc. It was possible, using a system of financial credits, to donate aid for the repair of churches. It was possible to send a car, or sometimes a replacement engine, or a motorcycle, or heating equipment, or washing machines for a seminary, or printing equipment. Secretly, and often with the recipient uncertain of exactly who in the West had heard of his plight and come to his aid, parcels containing everything from lump sugar and coffee to badly-needed medicines or liturgical books, would arrive at the home of a priest. Whole families were supported by parcels from ICCR and frequently the letters that came back would reveal that, because of the family's Catholic commitment, they had been in a desperate plight for years and unable to survive without help. Catholic young people who refused to join Communist youth organisations were denied places at university, and had to take menial jobs. Catholics who were active in some apostolic way often lost their jobs, and any social security benefits and were left destitute with hungry children to feed. For such people, aid from the West was a lifeline.

In 1958 Fr Werenfried launched the *Mirror*, a newsletter which would eventually be a bi-monthly publication in all major Western European languages and become a distinctive part of Catholic life for hundreds of thousands. For years, part of its special gimmick was that the front page was written in his own handwriting – distinctive, looped, firm and emphatic, it brought alive in vivid prose the plight of the Church in the East and the duties of those in the free West.

Fr Werenfried's theology drew heavily on the revelations of the young visionaries of Fatima in Portugal. As a result of a Marian vision in 1917, three young Portuguese peasant children spoke in dramatic language of a need for prayer and penance. Two of the children died not long after the visions, as a result of the worldwide flu epidemic of 1918–19. One, Lucia, survived to become a nun living in an enclosed order. The 'message of Fatima', which included a special plea that people pray for the conversion of Russia, had always been important to Fr Werenfried, and now he taught it repeatedly through his newsletters, speeches and preaching.

Children in Germany who had benefited from the sweets and food supplies given by the Bacon Priest were now, as teenagers, happy to respond to appeals asking that they in turn help others. A newsletter for children begged them not to forget the *Speckpater*. Helping him had in fact become a way of life for many.

In 1957 Fr Werenfried met Cardinal Stefan Wyzinski, Poland's heroic primate. He had been released from house imprisonment in a remote area and was now in charge of a Church which was united in its opposition to Communism but struggling to survive in a nation where there could be no hope of any effective uprising. There had been unrest in several Polish cities and there was to be more. The Church, while hoping for the day when Communism's yoke would be lifted from Poland's shoulders, meanwhile had to find ways to survive. Through Fr Werenfried, funds were available to train young men for the priesthood. There was no shortage of candidates, and the quality was high. But books, living accommodation, and funds for food and basic facilities were all needed.

Another Polish Bishop was also working hard for the Church – Bishop Karol Woytila of Krakow. In his diocese a massive new industrial and living complex was being created on the outskirts of the city. It was bleak and ugly, lacking all facilities except for towering blocks of housing and the obligatory statue of Lenin. The Communist authorities were adamant that this would be 'a city without God'. But as people moved into the new housing, they gathered for Mass in the open air on land where they hoped and prayed one day a church would be built. Over the years, Fr Werenfried's organisation would play a major role in ensuring that it was – and would also forge strong links with the charismatic bishop who would go on to become Pope John Paul.

But all this lay in the future. As the 1950s ended, Fr Werenfried found that he had a massive international organisation, complete with a warehouse that was always being emptied and replenished. In one corner stood a huge mountain of rock sugar from which supplies were cut and packed every day to send in innumerable parcels to the East along with other basic groceries for needy families. In adjoining rooms, sewing machines whirred as teams of enthusiasts made sheets, vestments, and shirts. Elsewhere, people stacked shoes – or helped to mend them. There were shelves and shelves full of clothing, sorted according to size and type.

The organisation now employed a large number of full-time staff, all working in the shadow of and within the sound of the bells of the great Abbey of Tongerlo where the community still carried on its rhythmic life of prayer. Abbot Stalmans, who had been a stalwart supporter of Werenfried from the beginning, had died in 1953, but Tongerlo continued to give full encouragement to the work that had been started and day after day trucks rumbled to the Abbey with supplies or left with parcels to deliver.

Now the aid was coming not just from Flanders but from Holland, France, Switzerland, Germany and gradually from other European countries. Fr Werenfried was known as a preacher and a writer. He could number several bishops among his friends and advisers and helpers.

What about his family? The van Straatens had always been close. He continued to be in regular contact with his parents. They were proud of their son – although, as he always recalled, 'My father, being a cautious and moderate man, was worried that I always seemed to be making promises that I could not keep, offering money that I did not have.' He was not alone in that. Werenfried's accountant felt the same. It became part of the legend. But somehow the money always came in and the promises were always kept.

His family was important to him in other ways. He visited cousins regularly, finding a welcome in their home. Their young daughter was Antonia. She bore a family name, having been named after Fr Werenfried's aunt, who was her grandmother. She later recalled, 'Fr Werenfried was part of my youth. He came very often to visit my parents. I was at home, and so I saw this huge, big man, all in white. When he came, he always had magnificent stories about refugees, and that impressed me enormously. It was in the beginning of the work – he had started back in 1947 ... He came and told my parents about his plans, but also about the terrible things he had seen in Germany. My other uncles and aunts, they were ordinary people and they spoke about everyday things, but when he came, he always had fascinating stories.'

Antonia – called 'Ton' within the family – also remembered that her mother would take care of Fr Werenfried's long white Norbertine robes, which could not be sent to an ordinary laundry. Within the family, Werenfried still used his own baptismal name of Philip, and so to his young cousins he was 'Heroom Flip' – 'Heeroom' being the Dutch familiar term for priests, as 'Father' is in English.

Relaxing with the family was one way for Werenfried to

unwind – and his life with the community at Tongerlo was also central to him. He was still keen on practical jokes. On one occasion he dressed up as an Eastern bishop and was solemnly shown round the monastery and treated with great deference and politeness before his ruse was discovered to general hilarity. On another occasion, he gave himself a small goatee beard and became a visiting organist – he was shown the abbey's magnificent organ and expressed admiration for it but could not be induced to play .... Beneath Werenfried the preacher, crusader, fund-raiser, and passionate defender of the Church there lurked the high-spirited country boy who had been a rebel at university and who had caused his stricter brothers some concern ....

Chapter Seven

Criticism continued of ICCR. In 1954 an article in the Belgian paper *Le Peuple* headlined 'Apostolat ou Camouflage?' argued that the Vehicles for God campaign was actually unpopular with some German bishops – using as evidence the fact that the Archbishop of Cologne had chosen, for his Christmas collection that year, the needs of Catholics in Japan rather than Fr Werenfried's work. (This was nonsense – the Archbishop remained one of Fr Werenfried's staunchest supporters and would continue so for years.) The story was picked up by France's left wing *Drapeau Rouge* paper, which opined that the whole aim of the work was a clerical plot to create a Vatican-centred united Europe.

In 1956 it was the turn of another Belgian paper *Germinal* which said that the so-called help to priests in the East was in fact financing political Catholicism in Germany: 'Must Belgian Catholics get themselves mixed up in such a way in internal German business deals? Many Catholic laity feel that the help given by Fr Werenfried shows no balance ... the German and Belgian currency exchange system through which office the money must go is protected by bank privacy agreements. A pity! One would like to know how much of Fr Werenfried's money goes to the needs of priests and how much to build churches and provide cars in the Protestant regions of Germany.' The article ended on a threatening note 'Our source tells us it will not be long before we get answers to these matters.'

Fr Werenfried had never made any secret of the religious nature of his work. Although much of the aid delivered was humanitarian in nature – clothes and food for needy families – it had a specifically Catholic and missionary basis. The German refugees needed help because their plight represented not only individual human misery but a threat to the future of the Church. If they remained bitter and disillusioned, in squalid camps and temporary homes scattered across Protestant parts of Germany, their faith was unlikely to survive. These and similar fears had always featured in Fr Werenfried's pamphlets and speeches. The aid given to Catholics behind the Iron Curtain was specifically to help them retain their faith and to build up the Church for better times.

Funds, in any case, continued to pour in. People gave generously, both in money and in kind. The warehouse at Tongerlo continued to be a focal point of the work, with staff working long hours and a continuous bustle of activity. Priests from behind the Iron Curtain sometimes had very specific requests: for spare parts for a car or for a typewriter, for certain badly-needed medicines or vitamins for a malnourished family, for books or catechisms explaining points of doctrine, for liturgical vessels, roof tiles, disinfectant, whitewash for walls. The poor economies of the Eastern bloc countries in fact made it easier to donate goods. These countries were so hungry for foreign currency that they accepted it even if the recipient was a priest who would thus be able to obtain items that he needed for urgent repairs to his church building. The work was expanding. In 1959 Fr Werenfried went to India. There was a link with Eastern Europe in this – one small nun who was working with the poorest of the poor in

Calcutta. She came originally form Albania. At the time
Fr Werenfried met her, she had been working for fifteen
years with her new religious order: she was virtually
unknown outside India. Some years later, news of her
work had spread and she was known across the world. Her
name was Mother Teresa.

Fr Werenfried wrote later:

'Mother Teresa's nuns and assistants search the
streets of the city to pick up the dying. They are laid
on biers and carried to the death house. One bier lies
next to another in six long rows. Mere skeletons
covered with a dry skin, waiting for death. Huge
black eyes stared at me fiercely. But Mother Teresa is
with them with her assistants. Probably for the first
time in their lives these dying people learn what self-
less love is.'

He noted that there were about 125 nuns, of whom
six were European.

There is a girl from Freiburg. Four years ago I
preached there. After the sermon she came to the
parlour and told me she wanted to dedicate her life to
God in the service of the very poorest, and could I
tell her where she could go? I honestly did not know.
I promised that I would pray for light and advised her
to discuss the matter with somebody who knew her
intimately. Then God would certainly show her the
way.

I never heard anything more of her. But in Calcutta
I recognised her in the house of death and she recognised me. She has been working there for a year and a
half. In the last few years they have been able to show
a little love to more then twelve thousand dying
persons. It is not so much the sari or the bowl of rice

but especially the motherly care that illumines their last days like a miracle.

The sordid reality of life in Calcutta hit Werenfried with a tremendous impact. After baptising a dying baby he accompanied the tiny corpse to the place near the Kali temple were bodies were burned:

There were seventeen trenches in the ground where a wood fire was burning ... The child was laid with the other dead people on the ground until a trench was unoccupied ... Children were playing with bones that had escaped the fire. A sacred cow wandered among the burning trenches and snuffled at the dead child. Now and again a dull explosion was heard: these were the skulls exploding. Every time a body was ready the ashes were gathered into a pot and thrown into the river ten yards further along where children in the water were splashing and playing with mud and ashes.

In this scene human beings are nothing more than a slab of flesh, a piece of bone, a heap of ashes. What is the reason why those people are still so little affected by Christianity after four centuries of contact with it? The reason is that we, Christians, have been criminally lacking in true love and brotherly help. This is especially the case with the Christian peoples, who, as colonising powers, have borne the responsibility for the development, the education and the religious instruction of the so-called under-developed countries. I know quite well that we should furnish the present-day Samaritan services which our dead ancestors of the colonial era cannot now supply.

He was writing prophetically. Very soon the work of his

own organisation was to expand dramatically, changing its name in the process, to include vast stretches of the world where the problem was not the Iron Curtain, or Communism, but massive human and spiritual needs.

In 1960 Fr Werenfried published a book *They call me the Bacon Priest*, telling the extraordinary tale of his adventures, beginning with the day he wrote his first Christmas appeal at Tongerlo Abbey for help for the German refugees. Perhaps he thought that the publication of the book would be a sort of testament that would record certain tragic facts for history. It was important that the massive scale of the expulsions under the Potsdam agreement, the atrocities in Communist countries, the misery of the poverty there, be recorded for all time. But things turned out differently. The book turned out to be more connected with the future than the past.

He sent copies to bishops around the world – partly because he thought that after reading it many would send donations towards his work. Some did. But mostly, they wrote begging letters asking for help. They told of the problems of the poor, the homeless, the refugees, the orphaned, and the distressed in their own dioceses. The crunch came with a letter from a Latin American bishop. It was good to know of the work that was being done for people suffering under Communism, he wrote. But could he put in a plea for the poor of his own diocese, which was part of the free world but so menaced by poverty, and by the huge gulf between the very rich and the very poor, that some day the people might turn to Communism out of sheer desperation? Why not help us now, he suggested – and save yourself time and money later on?

'This made sense to me,' Fr Werenfried was later to recall bluntly. 'I went to see him to find out what we could do.'

The work was, in any case, poised for expansion. Shortly before publishing his book, Fr Werenfried had made a secret visit, in disguise, to Eastern Europe. Although Stalin was now dead and some regimes had eased up from the reign of terror that had marked the dictator's rule, there was still no question of allowing critical visitors from the West to get a sight of the reality of life under Communism. A priest with the name van Straaten had no chance whatever of getting a visa to cross into any Iron Curtain country. Even seeking permission to obtain one could put the whole of the charitable work of the organisation in jeopardy.

The fact of the organisation at Tongerlo with its massive warehouse and its network of supporters across Western Europe was well known. Less known was how it operated. The parcels that crossed the borders day after day came from named individuals who had no official link with Tongerlo. The words 'Iron Curtain Church Relief' never appeared on any parcel or any dollar credit that went into any Eastern European bank account. The people who occasionally visited Eastern Europe on behalf of the organisation went as tourists, and made their visits to priests and bishops – who often did not know exactly who they were, but only that they were Catholics from the West – with extreme caution. It was unfair to burden the recipients of aid with too much information, which they might be forced to reveal to the authorities if they were put under pressure, or might reveal inadvertently. Thank you letters received from the East often revealed how secret things had to be: one schoolmaster said that his children often spoke about the 'mysterious uncle who sends parcels from a far country because he knows they are poor', and a priest wrote: 'Although I can say nothing to my parishioners of your noble deeds I have found a way to thank you: every day after Holy Mass we say a prayer for the intention of our unknown benefactor ...'

Even when he wrote his book, Fr Werenfried could not mention the parts of Eastern Europe that he visited, or how he got there. He was vague about how he managed to obtain a passport and a visa.

In fact, he obtained a passport by going to the Mayor of Geel, a town close to Tongerlo where mentally ill people lived. The Mayor, who knew of the Bacon Priest and his work, was prepared to give him the passport of a man whose illness prevented him from ever travelling abroad or wanting to do so. Armed with this, Werenfried then grew a moustache so as to look like the person in the photograph. 'It was only a small moustache,' he mused later, recalling it all. 'I didn't want a great big one like Stalin or Nietzche. Just something so that I would not look like Werenfried van Straaten.'

His trip produced dramatic material for his book and also gave him insights into exactly how necessary was the aid provided by his organisation in keeping alive Catholicism under the harsh conditions of authoritarian atheistic rule. He did not reveal his true identity to the priests and bishops he met, although he was able to give them information which assured them that he could be trusted. He was able to see for himself how money provided by Iron Curtain Church Relief had repaired church roofs or provided books for students. But he also saw how much more needed to be done. The local bishops and priests often fought long drawn-out paper wars to achieve permission to build a church or even to repair one. The work itself had to be done by volunteer labour and often at night. These were the least of the problems: young men studying for the priesthood went hungry in bitterly cold makeshift crumbling buildings, elderly priests died as they struggled to cover vast areas to allow people a chance to get to Mass just occasionally, heavy taxes crippled any attempts to raise money from church collections, the 'Peace Priests' movement was used by the authorities to divide and demoralise the Church. Illness, arbitrary arrests, lack of books from which to teach the Faith, hunger, the lack of news from the wider Church, all contributed to the pressure.

They call me the Bacon Priest became a best seller. It carried a foreword by Cardinal Josef Frings, the Archbishop of Cologne, who described Fr Werenfried as a man with 'a golden heart, full of humour and deeply sensitive, a modest and deeply religious priest and monk', and a 'herald of unconditional charity'. The book was translated into every Western European language and was bought by the thousands of people who flocked to hear Fr Werenfried preach or who subscribed to his newsletters. It was sold at parish events, passed around by sympathetic priests, introduced into parish organisations. It carried pictures of Fr Werenfried in the untidy warehouse at Tongerlo, or sitting on a table chatting to a crowd of volunteers during a break in work. It showed formal events such as the blessing of the Vehicles for God and – most popular and widely reprinted – an informal shot of Fr Werenfried in the pigsty at Tongerlo with a plump pig. It helped to establish the name of the Bacon Priest among English-speakers: previously the charity had not been well known in Britain but now it began to attract supporters, who could send donations via the Norbertine Priory at Storrington in Sussex.

The scene was set for expansion, and when it came, it was with vigour.

The name change actually began with pressure from Eastern Europe. Once it was clear that Iron Curtain Church Relief was too narrow a title – because aid was now starting to flow to India, to Latin America, and to refugees in Palestine, among other places – Fr Werenfried planned to change it to 'Aid to the Persecuted Church'. This seemed possible for a while. But then problems arose in Yugoslavia. This was then under the rule of Marshal Tito, whose government had the reputation of being the mildest and most outward-looking of all those in Eastern Europe. Certainly it was comparatively easy to send aid there, and several churches were being actively helped. Tito made objections to the Vatican when he learned the name of the organisation, stating emphatically that he did not in any way persecute the Church. There seemed little value in arguing the point. At discussions in Rome, Fr Werenfried willingly agreed to a new name: 'Aid to the Church in Need'. This seemed to satisfy everyone.

In fact, many in Germany still continued to call the organisation *Ostpriesterthilfe* – Help to the Eastern Priests – and this title still appears as part of the charity's name in that country. For many people, it was also just 'Fr Werenfried and his work' or 'The work of the Bacon Priest'.

Now began a series of overseas visits to places where poverty stalked and the Church was menaced not by Government decree but by the sheer scale of human misery. Fr Werenfried went to Hong Kong, then an overcrowded British colony to which desperate refugees from Communist China attempted to flock every day. Many died on the dangerous journey – many more were turned back by the British authorities at the point of a gun just when they were within sight of their goal. They simply could not be accommodated, even though massive housing projects were under way as whole chunks of the land were being scooped out and flung into the sea to allow for the creation of vast tower blocks. No child in

Hong Kong would ever play in green open spaces or enjoy gardens and trees – and some were forced by poverty to earn a living for themselves and their families by acting as prostitutes among the visiting sailors. Even worse was the plight of the refugees in Korea, living in squalor and sickness in shanties which would be deemed unfit for animal habitation. Then in Latin America, what he saw caused Fr Werenfried to pour out his feelings in an appeal to the great figure of Christ which stands with arms outstretched on the great hills overlooking Rio de Janeiro and its harbour: the poverty, the families living among the filth of rubbish dumps, the children doomed to die for lack of basic medical care, the open puddles of sewage, the hopelessness of boys and girls with no chance to learn to read or to earn an honest living, or to establish homes and families of their own in decent conditions.

As the *Mirror* newsletter sent these reports to Catholic readers in Western Europe, money poured in for new schemes – housing projects in Santiago de Chile, care for leprosy patients in Korea, support for desperate families in Hong Kong. Always, the aid was given to a local Catholic priest or religious order or charity that had work and plans in hand and needed only practical support to implement them. But, as with millions of hungry Germans packed into refugee camps on the outskirts of ruined cities in a defeated nation, the needs and suffering at times seemed quite overwhelming.

The headquarters was still at Tongerlo, where miracles of administration were accomplished using basic office equipment in rooms sectioned off from the main warehouse. There seemed to be no lack of volunteers to work under such conditions, even though the housing accommodation on offer was also pretty bleak. Fr Werenfried's young cousin, Antonia Willemsen, joined the work at this time.

I'd always wanted to work in theatre, but my parents weren't too happy about that. I became a teacher, but didn't really enjoy it. I remember thinking at one stage: 'Have I got to spend the rest of my life doing this?' Then I got a bit of a break – I had the opportunity of doing an audition for a theatre school, and I decided to write a piece of my own to perform rather than just choose a classic piece of drama to present. They really liked it, which was exciting.

Then the school where I was teaching had a drop in pupil numbers for the year ahead, and had to lose one teacher. That was me, as I had been the latest appointment. I wasn't sorry to leave, but I had to decide about my future. Without knowing about the theatre audition, I had written to Heroom Flip – that was Fr Werenfried of course – about the possibility of working for him. He didn't reply initially, and I was under some pressure as if nothing else came up I'd have to start applying for another teaching job before the new term began. Then he suddenly turned up at our home in his car.

Antonia – Ton – was amazed at her first encounter with the Tongerlo warehouse. 'It seemed to be in complete chaos,' she said. 'There were big piles of shoes, and stacks of foodstuff. Then there were compartments made of what seemed to be cardboard, sectioning off funny little offices where people worked. I can't adequately describe how muddled it all looked. But it was obviously functioning.'

The only real problem was that, although Tongerlo was just across the Belgian border from Holland and not very far from her home, the journey was an inconvenient one, involving two buses and two trains, a real trial in a cold

Dutch winter. She took on the job, but with some misgivings.

There was accommodation available for people working at the warehouse. We girls had rooms in the nearby town – but what rooms! We joked that it was sort of convenient, because you could lie in bed and glimpse the sky from the holes in the roof, and see what the weather was to be like that day ... but when it rained we had to dash about setting buckets in strategic places.

At one stage we had one lady who worked with us who obviously came from a rather grand family – I remember that when she first arrived, it was in a very smart Mercedes. She joined us in this grim accommodation and one night when it was bitterly cold she couldn't get out of the door at the back to use the loo because it was simply frozen up – and so she had to go out of the front door, and down the road, and round to the back that way ... it really was all rather primitive. Eventually, I told Fr Werenfried about it and I was called to the Abbey where the Abbot had a meeting with me and told me that he had some rooms we could use.

They were rather pleasant rooms, above the laundry, and warm and airy – but there was one problem. We would have to be inside, every night, winter and summer, by 8 p.m. – not allowed even to take a walk outside. We were really living virtually within the bounds of the Abbey itself so he did have a right to make this request, but for some of us it was all just a bit too strict. It would mean we could never have an evening out. Some girls were perfectly happy with this arrangement, but I wasn't – and it ended with me and Fr Werenfried walking through the town, he in his white habit and me trailing along behind, knocking on doors to see if we could find accommodation. I remember thinking that I knew how Mary felt when she arrived in Bethlehem and there was no room at the inn!

In the end we found rooms in a simply lovely house owned by a delightful lady who created a real home-from-home for a group of us girls. She was glad to have the companionship. There was a good meal waiting for us every night and we really settled in comfortably and were extremely happy there.

When the opportunity came up at the theatre school, Ton turned it down. Something about the work at Aid to the Church had gripped her. In fact, although she did not know it, this was to be a lifelong commitment.

Chapter Eight

In 1964 the work of Aid to the Church in Need moved to Rome. The warehouse remained at Tongerlo, but the headquarters and administration all went to offices in the city of the headquarters of the Catholic Church. This marked a change in the status of the organisation. It was no longer just a private initiative run by a priest with the backing of his religious order. It was now a 'Pium Sodalitium' of the Holy See, and Fr Werenfried was officially confirmed as General Moderator.

Much else was happening in Rome at this time. Pope Pius XII had died, to be replaced by Pope John XXIII. He had called an Ecumenical Council of the Church, which would become known as the Second Vatican Council, or, in colloquial shorthand, 'Vatican II'. Probably most of the bishops of the world who assembled in Rome in 1962 for the opening of the Council had absolutely no idea what would be unleashed onto the Church and the world under its name and banner. In fact there was a general feeling that it would celebrate and confirm a time of expansion and glory in the Church. The number of Catholics was on the increase everywhere. The Church was more than holding its own in its ancient heartlands of Europe, having survived the ravages of war and the lure of post-war material prosperity. It was on the march in Africa and Asia where the heroic work of missionaries won universal praise and the blood of earlier martyrs seemed to have been shed to good purpose as locally-born priests and nuns now swelled the ranks of officers in Christ's army and new churches and schools and hospitals were to be found everywhere. In North America and in Australia every town had its Catholic church and school and network of Catholic organisations. In South America Catholicism was woven into the very core of everyday life for rich and poor alike.

But Vatican II proved to be the catalyst that a number of people had long sought for implementing their own agenda. As the Council got under way, it became clear that massive tensions were evident as well-funded groups from Western Europe and North America sought to promote specific ideas ranging from the innovative – informal prayers and pop music replacing Latin and chant in the liturgy – to the downright heterodox such as attempts to change Church teachings on marriage.

Fr Werenfried's ideas – and his implementing of them – on the needs of the world's poor and the urgency of supporting the Church wherever it was menaced by hardship or by oppressive governments – were completely within the scope and message of the Vatican Council. But his voice was not among those which were dominant among the *periti*, the influence opinion-formers and lobbyists and campaigners who thronged to Rome during the sessions of the Council and had the ear of the bishops and the mass media. Concepts such as charitable aid seemed to be dull and worthy, while the notion of a new-style Church committed to a radical if ill-defined political agenda appealed far more, especially to secular writers in the media. It was pleasant to hear that the apparently immoveable Roman Catholic Church appeared to be shifting its ground – initially on things like the use of

Latin in the liturgy but perhaps in the longer-term on other issues where the teachings had proved tough to live out – the need for penance and confession, the importance of a regular prayer-life, God's laws on chastity and lifelong marital fidelity, the unique and irreplaceable role of the priesthood.

After Pope John XXIII's death the Council was resumed under Pope Paul VI. But its actual deliberations were to be of less importance in the immediate future than action taken and policies implemented in what was often termed the 'Spirit of Vatican II'. Under this slogan, thousands of priests and nuns and monks abandoned their vocations. Catholic schools destroyed textbooks and catechisms and opted for general discussion instead of structured religious teaching on the Catholic faith. Liturgy was in chaos as 'experts', often self-appointed, announced that it was necessary to jettison beautiful old vestments, sell off chalices, destroy church sanctuaries and use informal settings in coffee-rooms and youth clubs for Masses where the dominant themes would be pop music and the recitation of favourite poetry or readings from current political authors.

During the years of the middle and late 1960s when all of this was beginning to make its impact on the Church, especially in Western Europe, Fr Werenfried's eyes were largely focused on the needs of the poor, in parts of the world where these controversies barely existed. In 1965 he visited Africa, flying into Congo (later Zaire), where he joined struggling teams attempting to help groups of refugees to survive amid the horror of war and in a land where little food could be grown or imported because of the continual chaos and disruption caused by fighting and corruption.

Aid to the Church in Need was now deeply involved in Latin America, where projects of many kinds were now receiving funds. Funds were also going to Palestinian refugees in the Holy Land, to the Chinese in Hong Kong, to the victims of war in Korea and Vietnam. Every aid project involved human beings at stages of their lives where they were vulnerable, needy, and dependent on the love and decency of others in order to cope and survive. Hundreds of individual human stories poured into the headquarters of Aid to the Church in Need via the priests, teachers, catechists, sisters and monks serving these people. Letters and reports, poorly-written requests hand-written on cheap paper, pleadings produced on inadequate typewriters from bishops in poor districts – all conveyed pleas for help or requests that their plight be drawn to the attention of the wider Church.

The work in Eastern Europe still continued. In 1967 a journalist described 'this resourceful, audacious, deceptively amiable priest' who was sending extraordinary amounts of aid across the Iron Curtain:

> In the past few years, he has managed to supply to needy persons or groups in communist countries not only the staple commodities of charity, but also, among other things, seven invalid chairs, a small organ (plus spare parts), bells, gardening tools for old people's homes, sewing and washing machines, a concrete mixer, musical instruments, vacuum cleaners, magazine subscriptions, an apiary, a second-hand motor for a priest's 1944 Volkswagen (which he wanted to keep because he was afraid that a new car would attract the attention of the authorities), and a prefabricated house.

The article quoted Slovakian Bishop Paul Hniliicia saying 'Fr Werenfried's is the strongest and most insistent voice that has been raised to awaken people in the West to the truth of what is happening to the Church in the East. Nothing must be allowed to still that voice.'

In Rome, Fr Werenfried slept at the central house of the Praemonstratensian Order, but his real base was the office headquarters of Aid to the Church in Need. During these years in Rome, the work was consolidated and the newer commitments, to projects in Latin America, Asia, and Africa, were put on a firm foundation and became rooted into the life of the organisation.

Ton later recalled:

I loved the time in Rome. It was idyllic. For someone like me, who had grown up in Holland, life in a warm Mediterranean country was a revelation. I enjoyed every moment. In fact I wondered why any person would bother to live of their own free will north of the Alps.

Every morning I'd hurry to the office, stopping on the way for coffee and breakfast in a café – Romans don't tend to eat breakfast in their own homes. And it seemed that every evening I'd be meeting friends for supper in a trattoria. I don't really remember using my own kitchen at all.

I loved the informality of it all, the sense of being at the heart of things, the buzz of being in a place which brought together so many different sorts of people active in different ways.

But it has to be said that there were big disadvantages to running a major international charity from Italy. The Italian postal service! It was really hopeless – we had to arrange for a courier to collect our letters every week and take them to Brussels where they would be mailed, and at the same time pick up any

Johan, Philip (Fr Werenfried) and Gerard van Straaten at their childhood home, 1917.

The three brothers as priests: Amatus and Modestus are Augustinians while Werenfried had recently joined the Norbertines; 26 August 1935.

'These children are looking for their parents' – a poster in a church in post-war Germany. There were many such heart-breaking posters, as families dispersed by the war, tried to find each other again.

'Rosemarie' – the little girl whose plight as an expellee in 1945 moved Fr Werenfried to send her his special 'open letter' which revealed the plight of such German children.

German children in a post-war camp in 1947: many had lost one or both parents in the war or in the subsequent chaos of expulsion from Eastern Europe.

A scene in a post-war camp for German expellees (late 1940s): this seems rather posed and 'tidied up' and is probably a publicity picture, but gives some idea of the cramped conditions.

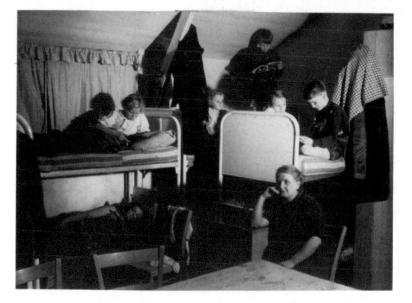

Post-war reconciliation: German children in Belgium for a holiday with
Belgian farming families, 1950.

A 'Vehicle for God' – Fr Werenfried preaching at a massive open-air blessing of chapel-trucks at Konigstein, 1950s.

Fr Werenfried preaching at the dedication of a chapel-truck, 1950s.

A chapel-truck in operation in the 1950s: German expellees from Eastern Europe gather for Mass.

The 1950s – chapel-trucks set off from Konigstein for the refugee areas.

Bundles of clothing being collected in a chapel-truck in Holland for the Church in Need in the 1950s. Some of the trucks were given names – this one has been dedicated in honour of the hero Croatian Bishop, Cardinal Stepinac, who died in prison in Communist Yugoslavia.

At Tongerlo – Fr Werenfried began the work of Iron Curtain Church Relief under the protection of this great Abbey.

'Offerings for the Bacon Priest' – Fr Werenfried on a fund-raising tour in one of the chapel-trucks in the 1950s.

An audience with Pope Pius XII in 1955.

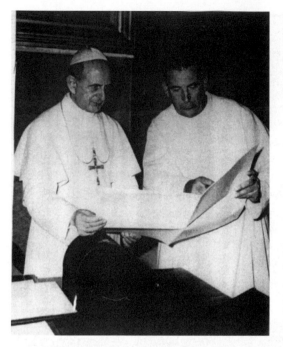

Pope Paul VI with Fr
Werenfried,
discussing the annual
budget of Aid to the
Church in Need.

1960s – The Bacon
Priest meets
Chancellor Konrad
Adenauer, leader of
post-war West
Germany – and shows
him his 'hat of
millions'.

A 1960s poster produced by the Italian section of Aid to the Church in Need, begging for help for the Church of Silence, the persecuted Church of Eastern Europe.

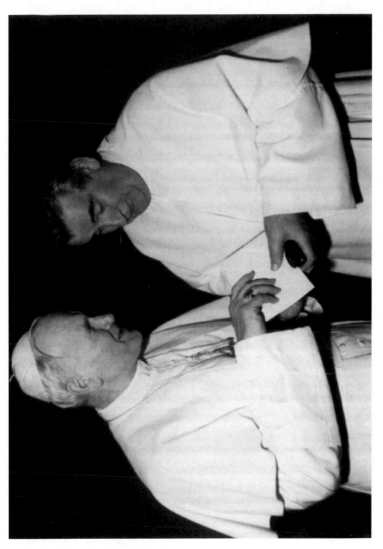

Workers together – Pope John Paul and the Bacon Priest in the early 1980s. It looks as though a donation is being handed over!

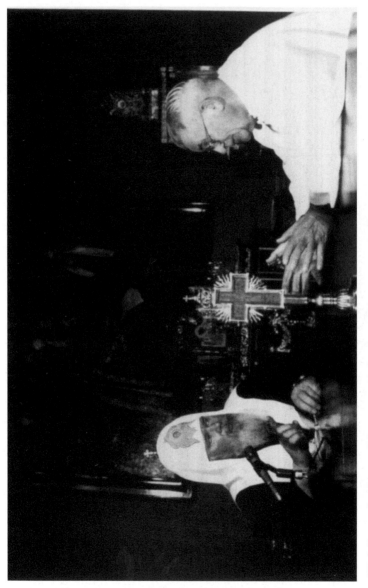

With Patriarch Alexei in Moscow on 13 October 1992 – a moment of history.

Red Square, 13 October 1992. Praying the Rosary in the heart of Russia as Communism falls.

Fr Werenfried and his team receive a blessing from Pope John Paul II on a visit to Rome, 8 October 1999.

Fr Werenfried with 'I Believe' – a children's catechism – the Jubilee Year project of Aid to the Church in Need, 2000.

mail from the postbox there. We couldn't get a telex machine – that's what everyone was using before faxes and e-mails came along, of course – installed. We couldn't get extra telephone lines. There was a problem with every trivial bit of office administration that was necessary.

Nevertheless, the links forged to Rome with the wider Church were useful and even crucial for the future of Aid to the Church in Need. And it was during these years that the worldwide commitment of the charity was established.

Fr Werenfried was later to set down some of his dramatic experiences in a book with the evocative title *Where God Weeps*. Certainly the tragedies that were being played out in many parts of the world in the 1960s were every bit as grim, and in some cases far grimmer, than anything seen in Europe two decades earlier.

> Yesterday I walked away in despair out of the mouldy hutch measuring 9 × 12 feet in which twelve people live. The walls are papered with the cover-pages of illustrated papers, pin-up girls in bikinis, pictures of St Barbara and Sophia Loren, of the famous Rio carnival and of the Holy Virgin. The tin roof of the flattened tar-barrels is not watertight. The air is rigid with stench and music. Flies and naked children crawl on the ground. Between this hovel and the next is a cardboard partition full of cracks and holes. Half-dressed young women peer from the window opposite. The huts are so close together that it is difficult to tell whether you are inside or outside! I walked out after a quarter of an hour and was sick in the open air like a dog ... (Rio de Janeiro)

This refugee camp is only a mile and a half away from the Simbas. It is estimated that about 50,000 people are still being held by them in the forest round Stanleyville. Anyone found with a tin of food or cigarettes is shot down for having had contact with the Americans. The terrorized population lives on nothing but manioc and leaves. Who can count the children who have died of hunger and exhaustion? Night after night they escape from the forest to get away from terror and misery. Many of the escaped families have lost more than half their children ... (Congo).

It is swarming with flies, cats and children. Here 70% of the population is infected with tuberculosis. The hovels are built on piles in the mud. The streets are higher than the built-up areas. They are floating streets. They are 16 inches wide and consist of rotting planks on top of water and filth. (Philippines).

But the important thing about the work of Aid to the Church in Need was that it could offer solutions. These might start in a small way, but they made a direct if modest impact and they had long-term objectives which were realisable.

In 1966 Fr Werenfried played a major part in the foundation of a new religious order for Africa. The 'Daughters of the Resurrection' was specifically for African girls who could not join any of the established religious orders because they could not read or write. It was essential to have a religious order which would bridge the gap between the educated and often Western-based missionaries and the ordinary African people Girls needed to have a vision of religious life which bound them firmly to their own people and to the needs and practicalities of the communities in which they had been born and brought up. With the tireless Mother Hadewych from Flanders, who had been working in Africa for years, a whole new religious order was born. Mother Hadewych was originally from the Order of the Holy Sepulchre. What could be more natural than to name this new order after the great event that emerged from the Sepulchre – the Resurrection?

The Daughters – in a very special sense, his own spiritual daughters – were to prove a constant source of joy and new hope to Fr Werenfried over the following years. With a distinctive but simple habit, much African singing, a great sense of dignity and grace in their worship, and enthusiasm as they tackled their training in catechetics, gardening and medical care, domestic management and child health, they were to breathe new life and hope into their own small corner of Africa. Mother Hadewych, as foundress of the new Order, would as the years went by see many many girls find fulfilment in this new way of life. In one sense, this was the same sort of development that had emerged in Europe during the Dark Ages, when religious orders were like beacons of light during times of political corruption, social unrest, and war.

Each new development was reported back to supporters of Aid to the Church in Need through the *Mirror*. Fr Werenfried's facsimile handwriting was now a familiar trademark, and the newsletter in its different languages was finding its way into thousands of parishes and homes across Europe. It was not just appealing for money. In fact, the financial aspect of the work became rather less important in Fr Werenfried's messages at this time. People knew that he was running an international charity, and they tended to give generously: there was no particular need to nag. The human interest of the stories he told – the do-it-yourself housing that transformed life for families in a shanty town in Brazil, the drugs and medicines for the sick, the cars and motorcycles that mobilised priests in the Andes and in Eastern Europe which meant that they could bring the Sacraments and the Mass to thousands more people ... all this had considerable human appeal. What mattered much more, at a deeper level, was a consistent message that prayer was still important, that the Church's message had not changed, that devotion to Christ in the Blessed Sacrament, regular confession, frequent recourse to the Rosary, were still central to Catholic life.

This was to become more important as the 1960s gave way to the 1970s and the Church faced an internal crisis which affected every active Catholic.

Chapter Nine

As the 1960s opened, it seemed as though these would be serene years for the Catholic Church. Although in danger from outside by ' persecution – especially in the Communist countries – there was an internal unity and even those persecuted were able to know that there remained a secure foundation for their faith in a Church which taught unchanging truths and expressed these through bishops who across the world were loyal to the Pope in Rome.

For Fr Werenfried, the opening years of the 1960s had been a busy time, with expansion of the work and development of his role within it. It was a time, too, that marked the passing of an era in his family; his mother had died in 1961 and his father in 1962. He had remained close to his parents and cherished their memory – for the rest of his life he would pray for them daily and keep their photographs, along with those of other relatives, living and dead, on the wall of his room. He retained good contacts with his brothers and sister and with his nieces and nephews. His two brothers who had preceded him into the priesthood had been with the Augustinian order throughout all these years. The family tended to take his increasing fame and occasional media controversies in their stride – the Dutch take some pride in having a phlegmatic and down-to-earth approach to life.

Even before moving the work of Aid to the Church in Need to Rome, Fr Werenfried had established good working relations with the Papacy. Both Pope John XXIII and Pope Paul VI gave general support to the work and were happy to be photographed with the Bacon Priest. Wherever possible, publications of Aid to the Church in Need would carry suitable quotes from bishops supporting the work.

Sadly, not all relationships worked smoothly. The realities of human personalities and misunderstandings intervened. There had been a rift with his Superior at Tongerlo, particularly over the raising of the status of the work with its own identity within the Church – not that the Abbot at Tongerlo had particularly opposed the move but there was hurt and resentment over the way in which it had been done and a perceived feeling that the organisation had rejected the normal procedures and the brotherly bonds of Tongerlo and gone 'over their heads' to Rome.

Sadder still was the controversy over the Building Companions, the men who lived and worked together as a community to build homes for the poor, chapels and monasteries as 'fortresses for God' and whose origins lay in the early days of the work in a ruined and hungry Germany. This religious movement, which Werenfried had created and felt was very close to his heart, was eventually removed from his control, something to which he would later refer as his 'bitterest moment'.

Over the years, many people would come and go among the staff at Aid to the Church in Need, some leaving in disappointment and resentment. It was not easy work. There was relentless pressure and sometimes unrealistic expectations. Some decisions seemed arbitrary, and sometimes a team spirit was hard to achieve among many creative and lively people, each of whom had chosen to join the work for his or her own personal and important reasons.

Interestingly, no one who left the work ever complained about the organisation's commitment to its tasks or complained of slackness. Nor were there ideological differences. It was as though the nature of the work, and its essential role in the Church, had a flow that was irresistible and would continue no matter what. But there were undoubtedly personal sadnesses, difficulties, and misunderstandings along the way.

Werenfried himself would always admit that he was not the easiest person to work with. He liked to describe himself as a stubborn donkey or a difficult and immoveable ox, or as a lone voice calling out an often unpopular message.

'When Werenfried set his mind on something, it was like a tank – he just rolled forward and went ahead with his plan, regardless,' said Ton. In 1970, after several years working for Aid to the Church in Need first in Belgium and then in Rome, she decided it was time for a change and she joined a Dutch government aid agency based at The Hague. There had been no disagreement with Werenfried, and no row – she simply felt it was time to take a different path. Her work involved researching aid projects for Latin America, and the style was certainly very different from that of a swift-moving Catholic charity run by a priest with a begging hat. 'I had to write virtually a book for each project, setting everything out in tremendous detail,' she recalled. 'And they were huge projects, involving something like a million guilders each. I enjoyed the work but stayed in touch with Werenfried – and of course there was still the family link anyhow.'

'I went with Werenfried and a representative of another

organisation on a trip to Latin America, and then later we met again in Rome. At one point he told me that he had a very good candidate for the position that I had held in Aid to the Church in Need. He hoped very much that his man would take the job – but if for some reason he refused, might I consider it? It sounded very unlikely so I said "yes". Then of course a while later I heard that this man had, at the last minute, had to pull out for personal reasons. I remember I told Werenfried "No!" very emphatically on the telephone. But I did end up going back, and I don't regret it.'

In 1970 Fr Werenfried was able to make a trip to Romania, after terrible floods there. His trip was a major breakthrough. This time he didn't have to go in disguise. A visa was obtained through the Romanian Embassy in Rome. It seemed possible that the Communist authorities were trying to show that a new era might be starting, with a new open approach to Church/State relations. News of Werenfried's trip was even reported in the press. The *Gazet van Antwerpen* Flemish newspaper ran a feature based an an interview with a member of ACN's staff, who confirmed that the Bacon Priest was travelling under his own name with the full knowledge of the Romanian authorities. Would he be able to go anywhere he liked? 'Yes and no. Nothing has been officially forbidden him. But he is watched day and night through the Securitate, the secret police ...'

The following year saw a trip to Latin America, and the year after that he was back in Africa, visiting Burundi.

But meanwhile, within the Church, the Second Vatican Council had taken place – and in its wake there were changes, debates, discussions and divisions which were to affect every part of Catholic life. Fr Werenfried had been active in Rome during the Council – it was a

A Life

good opportunity for him to meet bishops from behind the Iron Curtain as the meetings of the Council were the only chance to see them without their 'guardian angels' provided by the Communist governments. It coincided with the publication of his first book *They call me the Bacon Priest* and with the subsequent expansion of his work into new continents – Asia, Africa, Latin America.

But like other priests who remained faithful to the Church, he found the early years of the 1970s were difficult ones: the expression 'the spirit of Vatican II' was used as an excuse to abolish or belittle the central Church teachings, including belief in Christ's real presence in the Blessed Sacrament, the infallibility of the Pope, and the notion of an authentic tradition conveying truth that had been handed down inviolate from one generation to the next.

During these years, Fr Werenfried's messages in the *Mirror* became of increasing importance and significance. They became the focus for a rallying of faithful Catholics. Month after month, Fr Werenfried reminded people that the Church still stood firm on moral principles, that prayer still mattered, that going to confession was important, that the Rosary was a vitally important prayer, that God's Commandments had to be obeyed and the Church cherished and honoured.

The divisions in the Church ran right through his own family. One of his brothers took a path different from his own, and tended towards the 'progressive' faction within the Church – which in Holland meant that they were very progressive indeed. Reacting, perhaps, against too strict an observance of the Church's rules and regulations in the immediate past – the Dutch bishops in pre-war days had been renowned for their dislike of innovation and for the firm curbs they kept on anyone who seemed to stray from their approved line – there was now an explosion of dissident activity. It became the norm to oppose the Church's teaching on the wrongfulness of artificial contraception, the teaching on the lifelong nature of marriage, and the discipline of celibacy for priests.

At the personal level, Fr Werenfried and his brothers – neither of whom left the priesthood – never fell out. The human bonds remained firm and strong. But there were certainly things that were best left unsaid at family gatherings. Division ran deep in the Church during these years. It was ironic that the brother who had considered Philip to be the dangerous one, the rebel who was rather anti-clerical, was now himself in the faction that was opposing the Church's traditional line.

In 1968 when Pope Paul VI issued the encyclical letter 'Humanae Vitae', affirming the unchanging teaching that artificial means of birth control were morally wrong, there was a massive series of orchestrated protests, and huge splits in the Church were revealed by a fascinated mass media in the western world. In Holland, and elsewhere across the West, priests signed letters to newspapers disagreeing with the Church, they resigned from their orders, they launched newsletters and publications denouncing Church teachings. Many left the Church, and a good number of these married. All this coincided with liturgical chaos – old manuals of Latin chant had been thrown out (despite the instructions given at the Vatican Council that Latin was to be retained and have a special place in the Church's worship), new experimental ideas were endlessly produced for 'children's Masses' and 'youth Masses' and Masses with political slogans and Masses in coffee-rooms and around dining-room tables and virtually anywhere except with full solemn dignity at a High Altar.

It was easy to label someone as 'right wing' or 'left wing'

but in fact Fr Werenfried fitted neither of these descriptions. His work for the poor and his stance alongside them both in practical reality and in the printed word made it difficult to assign to him the image of a stuck-in-the-mud European-based elitist who cared nothing for the wider world. His passionate concern for the world's hungry and for the victims of war and oppression should have made him a darling of the left-leaning groups which flourished in the American and Western European Catholic church community at this time. But unlike these groups he was deeply involved with ordinary people in Africa, Asia and Latin America and knew that they cared little for political slogans from the clergy: they sought relief from hunger and they also wanted spiritual truth which gave meaning and purpose to life. His outspoken calls for generous gifts – free from left-leaning political rhetoric but rich in Catholic affirmations of solidarity with the poor and knowledge that God requires generosity from all of us – struck a chord with traditional Catholics and tended to make the 'progressive' ones uncomfortable. His continuing love for the Rosary, his consistent calls for repentance and for more prayer and devotion, his loyalty to the Pope and to the traditional teachings of the Church – and perhaps above all his unwavering conviction that atheistic communism and its oppression of the Church continued to pose a terrible danger – all made him an object of derision for those who sought to re-make the Church for a new era. But to others he was a hero.

For many thousands of faithful Catholics, the monthly arrival of the *Mirror* newsletter was a reminder that the Church would not and could not change her fundamental teachings, a call to holiness and to sacrificial generosity, a reminder of unfashionable truths about Communism and what was happening in Eastern Europe, and a source of spiritual strength. There was always news to tell: Fr Werenfried told stories of individual priests helped, churches rebuilt, food or clothing supplied to needy families – always with a human interest factor which made the events come alive to the reader. Often, the actual name of the country or the town or village could not be given as the recipients of aid would be put at risk. So readers heard about 'a convent in Czechoslovakia' or 'A priest in Lithuania'. But sometimes specific publicity could be helpful. In Poland, where the Church was strong, the Catholics very much wanted the world to know of the injustices they were suffering under a Communist government. They regarded their primate, Cardinal Wyzinski, as a national hero and in due course Aid to the Church in Need published his prison memoirs, written during the early 1950s when he was arrested during the time that Stalin had tightened his grip on Eastern Europe.

And while the work in Eastern Europe continued and in a sense was the core of Aid to the Church in Need at this time, work in Latin America was increasing. In 1974 Fr Werenfried launched 'Project AMA' in Brazil. The opening up of the trans-Amazon highway in that country had brought not prosperity but dislocation and the prospect of total disruption to the lives of the poorer people along the route. Fragile village economies were being disrupted and traditional ways of life destroyed while no real economic or social advantages were being gained. 'Project AMA' involved the shipping over to Brazil of 300 massive Swiss Army trucks which, by providing transport for essential services, would help the poorer communities to benefit rather than be hindered by the developments taking place in their region. The trucks were soon in use helping to ferry materials for the relief of destitute street children, providing transport links enabling employment to be provided, and giving whole communities control over their own lives and futures. A firm on the subject became a fund-raising tool across Western Europe – and also in Britain where, in these early years of the 1970s, Aid to the Church in Need was becoming known.

There were now local ACN offices running fund-raising and distributing material in many Western European countries: France, Holland, Germany, Austria, Switzerland, Belgium, Italy, Spain. In Britain, there had been a well-established link with the Praemonstratensian community based at Storrington in Sussex: donations to Aid to the Church in Need could be sent here and were processed and banked and the money sent on to support various projects. But now as the work expanded something bigger was needed: after visits to England by Ton Willemsen, a new lay director, Philip Vickers, was appointed and an office established in Chichester, West Sussex, with a Secretary, Sister Catherine Shakespeare, dealing with the letters and a small team of staff. Soon Britain was producing its own posters and brochures explaining the work of ACN, and selling copies of Fr Werenfried's books.

In 1975 the headquarters of the work moved from Rome to Konigstein. As we have seen, this was a place that had long associations with the work. Here the displaced German refugees from the East had found a home, and their spiritual leaders had been able to rally them. Here the rucksack priests had been trained and supported, equipped and helped. Here conferences had been held highlighting the plight of the persecuted Church under Communism.

The move from Rome was a matter of practicality: everything in Germany seemed to combine to make it easier to run an international charitable enterprise more efficiently.

'We labelled everything and packed things with numbers attached so that we knew exactly where everything would be put when we arrived,' Ton remembered. 'It was just extraordinary – everything went so smoothly. In fact, it was so much in order that Fr Werenfried and I were even able, three weeks before the move, to take a holiday. We knew that everything was in hand and that on our return we would find a new office established in Konigstein – and that's exactly what happened.'

'Looking back, I would say that the time in Tongerlo, those early years, was a time of improvisation. Then the time in Rome was a time of becoming part of the worldwide Church. And then the move to Konigstein was a time of consolidation and expansion.'

Chapter Ten

At Konigstein, Aid to the Church in Need moved into offices formed out of the old barracks that had originally been built at the end of the First World War and had been used after the Second World War for refugee relief projects. By 1975 there was little evidence of those post-war years. Germany was now immensely prosperous. Frankfurt had skyscrapers, a major airport, and the bustle of an internationally important city and financial centre. Konigstein, no longer a centre for refugees, was increasingly being seen – because of its picturesque beauty as it nestles among the hills, dominated by its own ruined castle – as an attractive place for Frankfurt's prosperous families to live. Successful businessmen sought to raise their families in a semi-rural setting within twenty minutes' commuting distance of the city.

The town of Konigstein now boasted a pedestrianised shopping centre with charming coffee-houses and restaurants. Its shops with expensive and attractive goods, and its travel agents and banks catered for the needs of a wealthy local community. In a quiet and almost forgotten corner of the parish churchyard, Bishops Kaller and Kinderman lay buried, after their years of service to their exiled communities. The refugee people whom they had laboured to help had by now long settled into the new West Germany, and the children of those first refugees considered themselves as West Germans, albeit with surnames and a family heritage which showed their roots in Silesia or Pomerania.

In fact the road that led to the new headquarters of Aid to the Church in Need was named Bishof Kaller Strasse, and in due course another adjoining road would honour Bishop Kinderman, who had been appointed an auxiliary Bishop of Hildesheim. Already, these men were fading into local history. The boys who flocked to the big Catholic boys' school that occupied part of the complex of buildings just off Bishof Kaller Strasse wore denim jeans and lived in a culture of pop music and easy travel, children of Germany's prosperous years. They were a long way, in culture, lifestyle, memories and experiences, from the orphaned refugee children who had been educated at the minor seminary in these same buildings thirty years earlier.

If the buildings themselves had many memories, the daily reality of life at *Kirche in Not/Ostpriesterhilfe* – as the signboard at the entrance proclaimed – was certainly highly up to date. In order to run a massive international aid programme with contacts across the globe, there had to be an efficient organisation, using everything that modern technology would provide in the way of filing systems, telephones, and office equipment. The staff included people who were fluent in several languages. There were different departments looking after the projects in various parts of the world. There was a separate publicity department, producing press releases and brochures. Production teams were also making films and there were the beginnings of what was to become a massive archive of historical material, telling the story of the Bacon Priest and the adventures of the early days and of the various projects from Latin America to the Congo.

The work at Konigstein increased daily, weekly, yearly. Now that the charity was part of the worldwide work of the Church, appeals poured in all the time for aid – to rebuild a church, give a scholarship to a poor student, mend a roof for a seminary. Not all the requests were genuine. All had to be sifted. A pattern was established in which aid requests were sent for checking with the local bishop, and investigations were carried out as to the feasibility of the project in question. The practicalities of life meant that the checking could not always be done according to the book. Some aid was still also being given secretly.

Letters poured in to Fr Werenfried from across the globe. By no means all were from people who asked for financial help. On the contrary – many of the letters enclosed a donation. For several years now, there had been a steady flow of donations from the grateful German recipients of his first gifts. People remembered that he had helped them during Germany's terrible post-war crisis and they thanked him in kind, with generous grants of money. With these letters – and the letters with gifts from all parts of Western Europe – came requests for a new sort of aid, the spiritual cry of people caught up in times of rapid change. People no longer wrote about post-war problems, the sufferings in a refugee camp or the anguish of having lost a husband or son on the Eastern Front. They wrote about a son who had left the church and was living with his girlfriend, a wayward daughter who was bragging about her use of the contraceptive pill. They wrote about priests who preached denial of basic Catholic truths from their pulpits, or who bullied them when they tried to stand up for old traditions. They wrote about their anguish when priests suddenly departed from the parish, having decided to spend their lives with a girlfriend. They wrote about their own uncertainties, asking whether what they had always been taught was still actually true, whether sacrifices made in the past had been worthwhile, whether the Church had gone mad or was still at heart preaching the same faith as before.

It was not just the Church that had changed. Post-war Europe had given way to something quite different. Pornography was now widely on display in supermarkets and newsagents across Western Europe. The widespread availability of the contraceptive pill made it seem as if there was no reason why sexual promiscuity could not be an attractive option. Britain was the first country to legalise abortion – in 1967 – and other countries followed in due course. Drugs were becoming popular for a generation which had grown up with peace and prosperity and found life dull. Cannabis, heroin, and LSD became substances that were part of youth sub-culture – initially just on the fringes of life for most teenagers and used only by pop-stars, but gradually infiltrating into the lives of the well-to-do and from them into suburban and rural life.

It was these sorts of issues that Fr Werenfried increasingly tackled in his messages in the *Mirror*. He wrote in an old-fashioned and forthright style. He begged Catholics to continue to entrust themselves to Mary, Mother of Christ and Mother of the Church. He used dramatic language to describe the menace that Communism still posed and the need for people to live as if the Catholic faith really mattered. People found his writings at once stimulating and reassuring. For many, this was a personal message from a priest they could trust. The distinctive style of the *Mirror* – Fr Werenfried's facsimile handwriting on the front page, news of the persecuted Church inside, with snippets of thank you letters from Eastern Europe and elsewhere – was a formula that did not change.

He was known widely as a preacher. The gimmick of his well-worn 'hat of millions' became more popular as the years went by, and when he stood by a church door after an appeal from the pulpit, the hat was always filled. Periodically, Catholic publications of the more traditional kind would run a friendly feature about this battling Bacon Priest who was always facing new challenges and helping new groups of people in different parts of the world. The more progressive publications never mentioned him. His presence, and continued success as a fund-raiser, preacher, publisher and crusader, was an embarrassment. It seemed likely that his particular version of Catholicism would, in any event, die out soon. He spoke frequently, for example, about the visions at Fatima in Portugal in 1917 and the haunting call to repentance they contained. He referred to the revelation that Mary had specifically asked for Russia to be consecrated to her heart. He spoke in apocalyptic terms about the eternal conflict between good and evil.

Although much of his time was now given up to Africa, Asia, and Latin America, the plight of Eastern Europe continued to have a special place in Fr Werenfried's affections – and in his writings. One of his greatest heroes down the years had been Cardinal Mindszenty. After the failure of the Hungarian Uprising in 1956, the Cardinal had taken refuge in the American legation, where he remained for the next two decades, a voluntary prisoner and a silent witness to the destruction of freedom in his country. He was a symbol of the Cold War, which saw the Communist nations of the East and the Western nations under NATO facing each other across Europe.

In 1973 Cardinal Mindszenty was given a new cross to carry – something so heavy that it seemed to his supporters, including Fr Werenfried, that it must surely have broken him. All during the years in the American Legation he had insisted that he was still Primate of Hungary, and he had known that the Church upheld him in this and was appointing no one in his place. Now Pope Paul VI took a decision: it was necessary to appoint some-one new who would be able to make some sort of workable arrangement with the Communist Hungarian authorities. He asked Cardinal Mindszenty to leave Budapest and come to Rome.

Fr Werenfried would later recall 'It can never be told how he suffered at the Holy Father's decision to remove him from office: 'God has tested him like gold in a furnace, and accepted him as a holocaust. That Cardinal Mindszenty did not fall to the temptation of justifying himself publicly, but accepted rather that the cross came from where he had least expected it was, when seen with the eyes of faith, the crown of his great life.'

It was no secret that the Cardinal believed with all his heart that the Pope was wrong. The Vatican *Ostpolitik* was in full swing: Pope Paul VI seemed convinced that it was necessary to find some new means of placating the Communist leaders and forging a new path for the Church in the years ahead in Eastern Europe. He appointed Cardinal Laszlo Lekai in Mindszenty's place, a man who was known as a theological conservative but who believed that the Church should fall in with the authorities of the nation, whoever they might be. Lekai had been Mindszenty's secretary and in earlier years had shared his imprisonment under the Nazis. But he lacked Mindszenty's clear understanding of the role of the Church and his sense of prophetic witness. Both Cardinal Mindszenty and Fr Werenfried believed that this was the wrong choice of candidate, that it sent a false message to the Communists and more importantly to the Hungarian people, and that, humanly speaking, it could not but harm the Church.

On arrival in Rome, the aged and exhausted-looking Cardinal was greeted by Pope Paul who put his own cloak around his shoulders. But the gesture could not mask the fact that the Papal decision had broken Mindszenty's heart – his obedience was a matter of the soul and of human will, but something which caused him an immense sorrow that was to remain with him during the few remaining years of his life.

Fr Werenfried was always sceptical of the Vatican's *Ostpolitik*. He believed that it was rooted in an ignorance of the reality of the Church's actual plight in Eastern Europe, a short-sighted belief in the inevitability of Communism, and a lack of faith in God's providence. It has to be said that he was to be proved right. And, as always, God's way of working things out was an extraordinary one: while at the beginning of the 1970s a Vatican-led *Ostpolitik* looked unstoppable, in 1978 the dramatic election of a Polish Pope stopped it completely in its tracks. It died dramatically, never to return, and it was Communism itself which instead crumbled and fell, with crowds announcing their own liberation in Prague and young people hacking away at the Berlin Wall at the end of the 1980s.

But all this was to be in the future in 1975 when, on Cardinal Mindszenty's death in exile, Fr Werenfried was invited to preach at his funeral at Mariazell in Austria. Enormous crowds attended – over 4,000 Hungarian refugees together with 3,000 other friends and supporters of the Cardinal from different countries.

It was clear to his hearers that Fr Werenfried, struggling like his hero to be loyal to the Pope, could only express his thoughts in terms of seeing somehow in all these events the mysterious hand of God:

For the Cardinal's decision, after a frank exchange of opinions, to obey the Pope had nothing to do with human diplomacy or Ostpolitik but formed part, I think, of the divine strategy of Christ.

Jesus Christ and all the martyrs who have shared His fate have gone before Cardinal Mindszenty along the hard way that he freely chose. It is the way of the saints of all ages. They are as deprived of their rights as was God's own Son, who took on Himself the form of a slave and became obedient to death on the cross. This cross of obedience is the basic law of Christianity. With all the praiseworthy and necessary endeavours being made to give greater importance to human rights within the Church too, we should harbour no illusions and never forget that we must try to be the defenceless disciples of Him who died as one without rights and who wishes to continue not only His life but also His death in each one of us.

That a giant of Church history like Cardinal Mindszenty submitted to this law is a sign of great holiness and an example to all who go bowed under the often heavy and sometimes incomprehensible cross of ecclesiastical obedience.

There was a prophetic note at the end of Fr Werenfried's sermon. He spoke of the 'hope of wonders which we pray that God may soon work through him [Mindszenty] for the rescue of His Church.'

These wonders were to start just three years later. Just when it looked as though the relentless Communist persecution of the Church would grind on for years – the imprisonments of priests and lay activists in Lithuania, the petty restrictions on church buildings everywhere, the banning of religious orders in Czechoslovakia, the censorship of all attempts at religious publications or public meetings, the creation of bogus Communist-front organisations to divide the clergy – something happened that no one could possibly have imagined.

When Pope Paul VI died in 1978 he was mourned as a decent man whose encyclical 'Humanae Vitae' had been the catalyst for massive disruption in Catholic life – an irony as he was at heart a liberal to whom the task of reiterating the unchanging and unchangeable teachings of the Church on sexual morality was not a major matter and not the thing for which he would have wished to be remembered.

His successor was the Patriarch of Venice, Cardinal Albino Luciani – a kindly, smiling man whose face became familiar as it was flashed on to the world's TV screens. He took the name John Paul – a dignified way of honouring his two predecessors. All seemed set for a gentle continuation of what had been going on for the past few years as a troubled Church slowly sorted itself out following a time of internal tumult.

And then came his sudden death after only a month in office – the stunned news bulletins, the stark headlines conveying the information, the bewildered Catholics filing into churches for their second Papal memorial Mass in weeks.

A second gathering of cardinals was held, and a fascinated world watched the Church go once again through the time-honoured rituals of a Papal election. By now, media fascination was beyond anything that had been known in modern times. Across the world newspapers and TV and radio programmes discussed and debated who the new Pope might be. Names of Italian cardinals were again tossed around, and their pictures flashed on TV screens as the merits, ages, talents and peculiarities of each were analysed. But the final decision of those voting caused media workers everywhere to start ferreting in odd filing cabinets and frantically telephoning obscure contacts for photographs and biographical material – the choice had fallen on a Pole, Cardinal Karol Woytila of Cracow.

He was of course known to Fr Werenfried, and was someone with whom Aid to the Church in Need had worked for years. When the Communist authorities refused permission for a church to be built at Nowa Huta, the ugly and gloomy steelworks township established on the outskirts of Cracow, it was Fr Werenfried's funds that made the building possible – and Polish courage and tenacity that got it built, with volunteer labour and in the face of police harassment and physical intimidation. The great church of Nowa Huta, modern in style, shaped like a ship and a towering presence in the dreary townscape of blocks of flats around the compulsory statue of Lenin, had become the subject of a feature film made by Aid to the Church in Need shown at Catholic parishes and schools across Europe.

Cardinal Woytila had even visited the headquarters of Aid to the Church in Need – initially bringing a request from Cardinal Wyszinski of Warsaw that future aid projects should all be channelled as one item through the Polish Bishops' Conference. It was clear that this was not in fact a policy with which the Archbishop from Cracow was in accord, but he was relaying it in loyalty to Wyszinski. When the request was refused – it was and remains the policy of Aid to the Church in Need to channel aid to each project individually, on its merits, and not be at the mercy of a national term of bishops, however worthy – there was evident relief and a rapport was established which was only to grow over the years.

Now he was in Rome. He took the name John Paul II,

showing a sense of continuation with his immediate predecessor and a gracious tribute to him. He addressed the crowd in fluent Italian. People were present from all over the world. When he addressed his own compatriots and spoke of his own Polish homeland, many wept. Across the world, watchers on television knew that an extraordinary new chapter in Church history was about to be written.

As Pope, he would bring to the universal Church something of the strength and sense of endurance that had been forged by the years of working under Communism. He would also bring the insights of a distinctively Eastern European Christianity – something sorely needed. From now on, the Church in Europe would, as he himself would express it, 'breathe with two lungs' – and recognise its heritage from both East and West.

The Communist authorities were caught off-guard. What could they do, as people took to the streets rejoicing and gold-and-white Papal ribbons decorated their doors and windows alongside the Polish national colours of red and white? Meanwhile the western media slowly came to terms with this extraordinary man who was at once a philosopher, a playwright and a poet, a pastorally-minded parish priest, a human rights campaigner, and much more. And the Church, too came to understand that a new chapter was beginning and that a dramatic break had been made with the immediate past. The Church was now looking beyond the confines of the 1960s and 70s. These were no longer to be the years 'post-Vatican II'. The next years were to be the years of Pope John Paul II.

Chapter Eleven

'Vatican Ostpolitik' was now over. The policy virtually changed overnight. No longer attempting to make compromises with the Communist regimes, the Church now spoke with a new confidence. Pope John Paul II went back in triumph to his homeland. Attempts by the Communist authorities either to stage-manage or to control events were really out of the question. Enormous crowds thronged the streets, cheered his arrival at every town and city he visited, jammed the public transport systems or travelled on foot to get a glimpse of him, packed out public squares and meadows and parks for his huge open-air Masses, and heard him tell them 'Do not be afraid!'

For Aid to the Church in Need this new Papacy opened up vast new possibilities for the giving of aid to Eastern Europe, just at a time when massive commitments had already been given to projects in every part of what was called the Third World – Africa, Asia, and Latin America. The only option was to increase fund-raising, and this was done. More appeals, more and better leaflets developed by the local national offices – and by now there were also conferences, meetings of national directors, training sessions for possible speakers and promoters of the work, targets to be met, big events to be staged.

The future of the work also needed attention. Fr

Werenfried began to talk about getting old, making plans for a time when he would not be around. Some sort of structure had to be established for the longer term – statutes, a President, and suitable committees. In 1981 a big meeting was held in Rome, with representatives from all the national offices, to begin work on this. There was a Papal audience, a general sense of celebrating the achievements of Aid to the Church in Need over many years – and some tension as ideas for the future seemed uncertain. In the end, detailed plans were shelved and Fr Werenfried continued to direct the work, as he had always done.

Although Fr Werenfried's links with Popes John XXIII and Paul VI had been reasonably good – he had had their blessing in his endeavours and his loyalty to each of them had never been questioned – there was no mistaking the change in atmosphere and attitudes between Rome and Konigstein with the advent of Pope John Paul II. Here at last was a Pope who understood the realities of life in Eastern Europe from the very core of his own experience. It was possible to discuss plans and projects with him and look to doing things on a wide scale. Here was a man who saw Communism as something that was not necessarily here to stay and which had to be accommodated, but as something transient, something that had wounded but not destroyed the human ability to seek and find the things of God.

Fr Werenfried's work seemed to take on a whole new strength in the 1980s. While he liked to shake his head over the fact that he had been called 'the last warrior of the Cold War', he in fact gloried in the title. He knew that many Catholics had disliked the attempts to reach accommodation with Communism, and that his own stance had been vindicated by events. But when he preached, it was not a question of affirming comfortable certainties. He challenged people with his questions about the West – its affluence, its collapsing morals, its denial of the place of God in the lives of men and women, its attempts to accommodate evils such as abortion, blasphemy, pornographic entertainment and the destruction of marriage as an institution.

He was still struggling with ill health. Busy schedules of travelling, preaching, planning and organising were interspersed with various illnesses. In the early 1980s a British Catholic journalist, Kevin Grant, had a memorable meeting with Fr Werenfried:

On an April evening in 1983 I walked with Ton Willemsen, general secretary of Aid to the Church in Need, into a small room in a hospital in Frankfurt. Sitting quietly in a chair beside the bed, in his white Norbertine habit, was the Bacon Priest, Werenfried van Straaten, then seventy years old. We were both a little pre-occupied with the following day. I was due to meet all his senior aides at Konigstein; they were to decide if I was the right man to become director of his work in England. Father Werenfried was due to meet a team of surgeons; they were bent on removing his gall bladder. Towards the end of my day of interviews Ton Willemsen sent for me. 'Father Werenfried telephoned just before his operation and told me "I want that Englishman to join". So do we. So will you?' It was the opportunity to serve a genius. I told her 'yes'.

Kevin Grant, who succeeded Philip Vickers at the British office of ACN, went on to be an energetic and dedicated director who also played a role in helping to develop the style and design of the publications produced. He eventu-

ally resigned to return to work in Catholic journalism and
publishing, while remaining a fan of the Bacon Priest. His
view of Fr Werenfried, written in 1987, gives a good
description of the man in the busy years of the 1980s:

> Cardinal Newman said that to live was to change and
> to be perfect was to have changed often. Father
> Werenfried tries, like all of us, to be perfect but
> admits to failing. 'I have a good heart,' he tells you,
> 'but a bad character.' How near he comes to perfec-
> tion will be settled in the courts of Heaven but the
> most powerful evidence of his genius is his power to
> change, to see forward, to adapt, to size the new idea,
> leaving beholders gasping. Another earnest of his
> genius is to bring good men and women, their gasps
> forgotten, following trustfully after him, their own
> hearts alight with a flame caught from his.
>
> Father Werenfried has never sought a sign. He *is* a
> sign. His genius has this further mark – a reckless
> reliance on the providence of God. It is not a reliance
> on spectacular interventions from above, but some-
> thing more prosaic, a reliance on the goodness of
> God's ordinary people. A certainty that 'people are
> much better than we think'. They are only waiting for
> a burning word to enflame their hearts. They are
> ready for heroism if we have the courage to ask heavy
> and difficult sacrifices of them.

Although the headquarters of the work was at Konigstein,
in the early 1980s the warehouse at Tongerlo, where
goods had been stored and packed and shipped to Eastern
Europe and elsewhere since the late 1940s, was still flourishing. It was a very important focus for many people,
especially the Flanders Catholics who had been the origi-

nal supporters of Aid to the Church in Need. Clothes and food, books and boots, all sorts of extraordinary items from sewing machines to priestly vestments, chalices to warm socks, had been checked and stored there and shipped on to needy and grateful people behind the Iron Curtain.

But things were changing. It was now much easier – and more useful – to send people cash donations so that they themselves could buy what was needed. And the expansion of the work into the Third World meant that European clothing was not so useful any more – people in Africa did not need warm coats or thick jerseys, and sending them clothing of any kind all the way from Belgium was an imprudent waste of funds that could be given directly to the organisers of projects on the spot. Packing, shipping, and customs duty costs were all part of the picture. The usefulness of the Tongerlo warehouse was coming to an end.

It was in many ways a sad day when, in 1985, this large store of goods and centre of activity at Tongerlo was closed. Here some of the great dramas of the early days had been played out. From here, parcels of groceries had crossed the Iron Curtain to bring hope and help to families in Communist countries. Here, helpers had been forged into teams which worked with extraordinary energy and commitment, during the Hungarian crisis of 1956 and the days that followed. Here all sorts of people found a home – Fr Werenfried had listed some in his *Bacon Priest* book:

Here in the warehouse is the kingdom of Staf and Fouche and Jan and Miel, Heinz and Stafke, Juul, Dietmar and Luigi, of Franske and Frans, Sus and Sooi, Guy, George and Gust, Bill, Rene, Remi and

Richard and all the sturdy fellows from East and West who passed through these halls or stayed there, who would have neglected their health or their families if the little manager Father Kets, or myself, had not sent them to bed on time, or driven them home .... Nothing is unimportant here. Nobody is superfluous. Everyone has found and can find a task in the service of this strange enterprise. Here Tuurke is sorting his shoes and Mr Savate his medicines. Here Miel counts the bales in the warehouse and the diners in the canteen. Here Werner, the old submarine sailor, repaired amplifiers, film apparatus and engines until he disappeared just as mysteriously as he came. Here Clement built stairs, dormitories and new offices with the same industry as that with which he once built churches, houses, and air-raid shelters. This was Leo's place, where he restlessly hurried to and fro for his export licences, his work schedules, his transport service, always trying to master his emotion and his nerves. Here Mariette filled in piles of forms for the collection service, for car insurance and for the cow killed by a chapel-truck ... Where are they now, all these faithful souls who spent their best years here, the tough fellows who came from the Foreign Legion or from prison, the idealists and the scatter-brains, troublesome people spoiled by sorrow and failure, the quarrelsome ones and the drinkers, the unselfish and the profiteers, the artists and the saints? These and many others helped us and sometimes hindered us to the limit of their capabilities, but whom we could not have done without, and to whom we remain grateful.

And now, not without some heartache and some controversy among people who had known this place over the years, the warehouse at Tongerlo closed. The focus had moved elsewhere.

In 1979 – still, at that time, using Tongerlo – Fr Werenfried had launched the 'Child's Bible' campaign. This was the year that the United Nations had designated as the 'International Year of the Child' – and Aid to the Church in Need saw this as an opportunity to focus on the needs of children and to fill a very specific need within the Church. 'Liberation theology' was being taught and promoted in Latin America by speakers who preached a political Gospel announcing that the priority was not to focus on God, His laws, and His promises, but on the formation of community groups for political struggle. For this, they needed new versions of the Bible which emphasised a political rather than a grace-filled message. Pre-empting them, and serving the practical needs of poor families, schools, and parishes where the children desperately needed good reading materials, came the 'Child's Bible', an attractive bright red paperback, brightly illustrated in a modern and vivid style, telling the salvation story and bringing alive the figures of Abraham, Isaac and the rest, showing how the Old Testament came to fulfilment in the New.

'La Biblia del Nino', initially created for Latin America, became a massive international project and over the next years would be translated into dozens of languages and find its way into countries across Africa, Asia, Europe and the Americas. People in Western Europe could buy a copy and know that their donation had allowed the book to go to a child in Brazil, Russia, Lithuania, or India. And in Western Europe the book had its own value – people discovered that here was a useful and authentic children's Bible which did not water down the message of Christ's Divinity or downplay the saving message of His life and His Church. The book became immensely popular as it was bought by parents, grandparents, godparents, parish priests and catechists. In poor countries, and behind the Iron Curtain, it proved its worth over and over again. For some children in Latin American shanty towns or in poor villages in Africa, it would be the only book they owned throughout their childhood, and much loved and cherished. Twenty years after its launch in the International Year of the Child, the Child's Bible is still flourishing on a gigantic scale, with 34 million copies having been distributed in 115 languages and in more than 80 countries worldwide.

As the 1980s opened Fr Werenfried's position moved from being that of a lone crusader or maverick priest into that of an established figurehead of a recognised international charity. In 1982 he was honoured by the Federal Republic of Germany. He had received earlier German decorations and was now given the Great Order of the Federal Republic in thanks for all that he had done for that country since the late 1940s. This ribbon and medal joined others from Austria and from his own native Holland – he was decorated with the Order of the House of Orange in 1981 at a ceremony in Rome, when the Dutch Ambassador to the Holy See made the presentation, thanking Werenfried for his work for Dutch-German friendship and reconciliation.

He was still writing the *Mirror* newsletter regularly: for many Catholics this was vital spiritual food and it was mailed using the latest computer technology to thousands and thousands of addresses on lists that were constantly being updated and amended. At every appeal for Aid to the Church in Need, by the now vast army of preachers and appealers, forms would be distributed on which people could complete their names and addresses so that they could receive this newsletter.

A vast array of other material was also now available from Aid to the Church in Need. From the start, there had been posters, booklets, handbills and leaflets. Now the organisation was using films and slides – soon there would be videos. In addition to collecting cash and cheques, it was possible to donate with bank cards. People had long been leaving money or property in their wills to Aid to the Church in Need, and this was much encouraged with information and forms available for the purpose.

At the heart of it, there remained this extraordinary Norbertine, with his vigorous preaching style and his strangely up-to-date – though so often denounced as out-of-date – message. Fr Werenfried had long been deeply caught up in the importance of the message of Fatima – the mysterious messages imparted to three young Portuguese country children in 1917 by a 'beautiful lady', identified as Our Lady herself, from Heaven who urged them to prayer and penance. By the 1980s this 'Fatima message', which had been popular in Western European and American Catholic parishes in the 1940s and 50s, seemed to many to be stale and irrelevant. But Fr Werenfried remained convinced that it was of enormous significance – and he was to be proved right.

Fr Werenfried had consecrated the work of Aid to the Church in Need to Our Lady of Fatima in 1967 during a pilgrimage to the shrine in Portugal of ACN staff and supporters, where a Mass was celebrated by Cardinal Josef Beran of Prague, in the presence of Bishop Kinderman of the German refugees and two other bishops exiled by the Communists, Bishops Malanchuk and Sloskans. Over and over again, in the *Mirror* and in his talks and sermons, Fr Werenfried spoke of Mary's call for the conversion of Russia, for the need to pray the Rosary and to heed the specific call of the young Fatima visionaries who had urged that faithful people should pray and do penance on behalf of poor sinners in order that God's message could be spread and His plans accomplished. It seemed as though Fatima held the secret of the events of the late twentieth century – the Second World War and its aftermath, the spread of Communism across Europe, the persecution of the Church in so many countries.

If the Fatima message was no longer heard by many Catholics in the West – except for ACN benefactors who read about it a great deal and were glad to be associated with it in prayer and action – it was most certainly held in great importance in Eastern Europe. Here, the message that Mary had called for prayers for the conversion of Russia, and for that country to be specially consecrated to her heart, was of immense significance.

On 13 May 1981 Pope John Paul was shot, at virtually point-blank range, in St Peter's Square in the middle of a great public audience. He had with his usual open style been out among the crowd, reaching out to people and greeting them. The bullets hit his stomach and he collapsed into the arms of a supporter, his face contorted with pain. Captured on film, the image of this savage attack gripped the world. It was the anniversary of the first apparition at Fatima. John Paul II was later to attribute his astonishing recovery from what should have been a fatal bullet wound to the intercession of Our Lady of Fatima. Certainly the intention to kill him had come from somewhere deep within the Communist centres of decision-making. And as he himself would later put it: 'One hand fired the bullet, another guided it'. Mary had come to the aid of one of her children – one who had always shown her special devotion. Later, the Pope was to go to Fatima and to crown the statue of Mary with a new crown in which the bullet removed from his body was embedded among the jewels. From now on, no Catholic could perceive the Fatima message to be old-fashioned, irrelevant or belonging only to the fringes of the Church.

Fr Werenfried preached the message of Fatima as part of his whole understanding of the unfolding of God's plan through history. To co-operate with God's plan, it was only necessary to do what Christians had always been asked to do – to live unselfishly, care for the poor and homeless and hungry, love and serve God, obey His Commandments, do penance for sin, pray. Aid to the Church in Need was first and foremost a spiritual movement, he insisted. He asked for alms because the poor needed help, and because God needed the co-operation of His children in the spreading of His truth across the world He had created.

With this emphasis on the Fatima message came a renewed campaign, increasing throughout the 1980s, against the collapse of everyday family and personal morality: the widespread acceptance of abortion, of divorce and remarriage, of sexual activity outside of marriage, and – increasingly as the decade went on – of 'gay rights', of easily available pornography, of forms of sex education for children which urged them into sexual experimentation.

Fr Werenfried was in a position to speak out in a way that few other priests could. As head of a massive international Catholic charity, he had earned the right to speak. The dollars, deutschmarks, liras, francs and pounds that poured into the offices of his charity across Europe went to help the poor of the world, notably those in the forgotten and unfashionable places. Equally, the letters that he received told him of the confusion and unhappiness in the hearts of many Catholics and he was staunchly with Pope

John Paul II in affirming that this confusion required a coherent presentation of the Catholic faith in all its fullness.

He often spoke about the apocalyptic vision presented in the last chapter of the Bible, of the Woman and the Dragon. He saw the role of Mary as central in Salvation history, and identified her profoundly with the fate of the Church in a twentieth century which had seen such tumultuous events in war, the uprooting of people from their homes, the imposition of atheistic regimes in nations that were once Christian heartlands, and the collapse of morals in the free parts of the world. As the end of the 1980s arrived, and it was only twenty years to the end of the century, how would things develop?

Chapter Twelve

And then came 1989 and the collapse of Communism in Eastern Europe, and the end of the Iron Curtain, the destruction of the Berlin Wall, the extraordinary events in Russia and the end of the Soviet Union.

This is not the place to go into all the details of these events – but as they slide behind us into history it is important to note that most commentators will probably note the visit of Pope John Paul II to his homeland immediately after his election as Pope, and the subsequent emergence of the Solidarity movement, as the catalyst that started the great unravelling of the Communist empire. It was a corrupt and hopelessly inefficient system which had been propped up only by its secret police and its military might. For years, ordinary people in Eastern Europe had swapped jokes about the everyday hardships of their lives and the luxuries enjoyed by the nomenklatura, about the constant lies told by the official television and radio stations and State-owned newspapers, about the dreariness of it all and the apparent impossibility of its ever changing. When the people of Prague emerged into the streets, jangling their keys and calling for change, creating a 'velvet revolution', the free world watched in awe and thrilled to each development. The Communist authorities were toppled and in what seemed an almost miraculous way, a genuine popular movement emerged

that finally put Vaclav Havel, the playwright and promi-
nent civil rights activist, in power as President. He spoke
of his nation as being at the spiritual crossroads of Europe,
and of needing to learn from its past heritage of spiritual
truth. It was the sort of language that Fr Werenfried had
been using for years. Alas, it was not the only language
that was being used as Eastern Europe and the former
Soviet Union struggled to be free from the Communist
past and from the racial and social and economic tensions
and frustrations bequeathed by geography and history.
War as Yugoslavia broke up into its individual nations,
street fighting in Romania as the last Communist ruler
tried to hold on to power there, the emergence of criminal
mafia gangs running whole areas in Russia ... all this was
part of the post-Communist reality as the 1990s
proceeded.

Aid to the Church in Need was to play a crucial role in
rebuilding the Church in all the former Communist countries – a role that continues. In the early years of the
twenty-first century, this role will be crucial. And, just as
Fr Werenfried and a band of friends had been at the
centre of Budapest during the Hungarian Uprising, and
later used radio to bring news of the Uprising to the world,
so he was present in Russia at a crucial stage of her
history, and was able to use radio to send a powerful
message, this time across Russia itself. In fact the story of
the part played by Aid to the Church in Need in the
dramatic events in Russia was quite extraordinary, as we
will see.

Within Eastern Europe, the speed of events as
Communism collapsed took everyone, including the staff
at Aid to the Church in Need, and Fr Werenfried himself,
by surprise. All events in the Eastern bloc countries had of
course been monitored for years, and with increasing

activity throughout the 1980s. One of the major projects
funded by Aid to the Church in Need was Keston
College, a study and research institute founded by an
Anglican clergyman, Michael Bordeaux, in the 1960s.
Michael, who sat on the board of the British branch of
ACN – the only non-Catholic to be a board member
anywhere in the organisation – had become interested in
the plight of Christians in Russia back in the days of
Khruschev, following a visit to Russia. He had begun
documenting their plight and trying to help them,
running a small organisation from his home in Kent. In
due course this expanded to become a major centre of
research based in premises that had once been a village
school on Keston Common. From this unlikely setting,
top-quality briefings on developments in all the Eastern
European countries were regularly sent to British and
other newspapers, religious organisations, human rights
groups, and Government institutions. Like Aid to the
Church in Need, Keston was regularly attacked for being
frantically right-wing, militantly anti-Communist, or
behind the times. In fact, it was to prove that it was well
ahead of most western news-gathering organisations and
showed a profound awareness of the human and political
realities of life in the Soviet-dominated world.

Thanks to Keston and to its links with all sorts of
people, from bishops to human rights activists, in the
Communist-dominated parts of Europe, Aid to the
Church in Need had an understanding, denied to many
official and Church organisations in the West, of what
was really going on in these areas. Fr Werenfried had
always believed that Communism would one day crumble.
His main anxiety had always been to plan and prepare for
that day so that the Church would be ready to fill the void
and offer people real hope, creating not only the basis of

an infrastructure of parishes and Catholic welfare networks and means of communication, but also and much more importantly a base from which a message of realism and practical Christianity for the future could be established.

When Mikhail Gorbachev became the Russian leader and announced the policy of *glasnost* or openness, Eastern Europe took him at his word. Groups which for years had been working for human rights and for religious freedom started to become more forthright in their agitation. Newsletters such as the Chronicle of the Lithuanian Catholic Church which had been systematically documenting human rights abuses, were now being circulated quite widely in the West and Lithuanians openly began to call for freedom for their Church and for expressions of traditional Lithuanian culture. Soon television viewers in the West were seeing things that at one time would have been unimaginable – huge public gatherings in the capital cities of the Baltic states and successful pleadings for the reopening of closed churches and cathedrals. Western commentators tended to get things wrong when trying to analyse this. One BBC reporter described such a rally in Vilnius, Lithuania, as 'an exercise in popular Communism'. It wasn't. It was the launch of a public and nationalist movement which was fundamentally anti-Communist and was to end in the freeing of Lithuania from Soviet rule and the re-establishment of the nation as a sovereign state.

In 1990, with Russia still officially Communist and the Union of Soviet Socialist Republics – including the Baltic states of Latvia, Lithuania and Estonia – still in place – Aid to the Church in Need organised a massive congress to look at events in Eastern Europe and to plan for the future. The theme was 'Persecution, Freedom, and

Rebirth', and the list of speakers was extraordinary, showing how rapidly things had changed and were changing in Eastern Europe. Speakers reported from Ukraine, where the martyred Eastern-rite Catholic Church was beginning to emerge from the catacombs to which it had been consigned by Communist persecution for three decades. A bishop from Slovakia's underground Church came to tell his story – and to celebrate the fact that he was now able to preside openly over his diocese and to rebuild, almost from scratch, a Catholic parish system and normal church life. Bishop Alexandru Todea came from Romania, with chilling descriptions of the persecution of the Greek Catholic Church there, of his own years in prison and the hopes and fears that new freedoms offered. There were speakers from Belorus, from Lithuania, and from Hungary.

Numbers were greater than could be accommodated at Konigstein so speakers and delegates stayed at Schonstatt, a major Catholic centre not far from the Rhine. Here in unforgettable March days in 1990, supporters of ACN who for years had worked, rallied, raised funds, prayed and lobbied on behalf of their persecuted fellow-Christians in the Eastern bloc, met these people and heard their stories. There were powerfully moving moments, as when Bishop Todea described the humiliation and horror of hunger in prison – the longing for 'a cup of tea or a glass of milk, the overwhelming desire to eat a piece of fruit, an onion, some salad, a piece of bread ... being deprived of the means of staying alive for an extended period of time awakens a hunger which is so dreadful in its mercilessness that it is only understood by those who have experienced it.' Or when Bishop Jan Korec described how he was secretly consecrated in 1951 and trained underground priests while working as a labourer and later as a night watchman. Or when Fr Imre Kozma from Hungary spoke of a nation that needed a whole new vision because of the horrors inflicted on it over the last forty years: 'Before solving social problems, we must first and foremost give priority to strengthening the faith, the joy at being alive, morale in the workplace – in a word, encouraging hope in the future.'

Fr Werenfried was in his element. In a major speech he outlined the plans for the organisation as it embarked on assisting with the massive task of rebuilding the Church in Eastern Europe. Given the extraordinary events that had taken place across the Eastern bloc, he could perhaps be forgiven for a slightly exultant note. He spoke of Mary and of Fatima, of the work of Aid to the Church in Need, then in its forty-third year, of his own frailty and mistakes and of the immense possibilities ahead: 'In drawing up our relief programmes, it is not what we can do, but what we should do, that must be decisive. For we can do all things in the power of Him who strengthens us ...'

But he sounded a warning note, which had also been echoed by other speakers. No one really knew what was happening in Russia, where Communism was still officially the ideology and Gorbachev was in charge, wielding power and swivelling events to suit his own purposes wherever he could.

> Communism is not yet a thing of the past. Do not let yourselves be carried away by the vain hope that Gorbachev will bring salvation. Certainly he is a transitional phenomenon and thus an instrument of Divine Providence, but perhaps he is no more than a trump card in the hands of those who really wield the power and have no intention of renouncing communism ... Have no illusions! ...

The essential note of the conference, however, was one of practicalities:

> Now that the red dictatorships are finally crumbling, there is an enormous vacuum in large areas of Eastern Europe – an empty space, without priests, without the Sacraments, without evangelisation. Almost everywhere, except in Poland, there are no seminaries, the religious orders are decimated and the surviving priests are weary, old and exhausted.

There was a desperate need for vocations – young people from the West would be needed, to join those in the East to work for revival. And the seeds of renewal, although present, were not easy to find and needed careful nurturing. Ordinary people, especially the young, in Eastern Europe, wanted to find some meaning in life and this could not be given with slick slogans:

> They are neither communists nor socialists any more, nor fascists either, but at the same time they are not yet Christian – by a long way. As yet they have no name. They are 'what comes after communism' ... They thirst after justice, freedom, love and truth – in a word after all those things of which communism has been the negation. But let us not deceive ourselves! 'What comes after communism' cannot automatically be incorporated into the Church. In order to win those who in their hearts have rejected atheistic materialism, Western Christianity must renounce its own materialism. As long as we have not succeeded in doing so, we shall have nothing to teach our brothers and sisters in the East.

This was no triumphalist message but a profoundly common-sense look at the realities of life in the world as the old East-West barriers across Europe were falling. It was to be the message to which Fr Werenfried would devote his final years: the need for spiritual renewal, for a genuine revival of Catholic belief and life, in the West as well as in the East. Aid to the Church in Need had always seen itself as being at the crossroads of the Church, where those who needed help received gifts from those with generous hearts. But this crossroads was also a vortex which showed up fault-lines and failings in East and West alike. The crumbling Church of the West, with its priests who had abandoned their vows, its silly leanings towards outdated Marxism, its liberation theologians and its ignorant youth deprived of fundamental religious instruction, was in no position to make grandiose plans for reviving the Churches which had survived persecution across Eastern Europe.

Among many specific actions agreed in 1990 was an extension of the already highly successful radio broadcasts to the Soviet Union. Already, since *glasnost* had made it possible to broadcast without being jammed, thousands of people were responding every week to regular radio programmes which went out to Ukraine and the USSR. They could write to a given address for Bibles and other religious literature and a staggering 90,000 had done so, stretching the capabilities of the campaign organisers at Konigstein to their limits and initiating the creation of a whole vast new department. Now, more was planned. Fr Werenfried liked to quote the prayer 'Rorate coeli ... Show, O heavens, from above and let the skies rain down righteousness.' Radio, and eventually television, would play a major part in the re-evangelisation of the USSR and its satellite states.

Initially, the plan was that this would be done in co-operation with an American Catholic TV station run by Mother Angelica, a doughty nun who had launched her own TV system after realising the damage that was being done to the faith of ordinary Catholics both by mainstream television and by the extremist Protestant sects. Mother Angelica's Eternal World TV Network had begun in a converted garage in Alabama and gone on to become a popular and much-loved nationwide TV station which was to engage the loyalty of millions and be a major part of American Catholic life. In 1990 it seemed possible that this would be an ideal medium through which Russia could be reached. But these plans fell through. Although EWTN was to go on to become a worldwide network and a huge and still-growing success, the relationship with Fr Werenfried foundered and eventually Aid to the Church in Need made its own plans. As with so many other projects, human failings and misunderstandings were always to be a part of the work.

After the 1990 congress the expansion of the funding towards projects across Eastern Europe proceeded apace – and developments in Russia were watched carefully for the great moments of opportunity which were certain to arise.

In 1991 Fr Werenfried made his first journey to the Soviet Union for the return of Cardinal Lubachivsky to Ukraine. There were extraordinary scenes as Ukrainian Catholics, so long deprived of their religious rights, acclaimed their Primate and affirmed that they had not forgotten or abandoned their traditional Faith. 1991 was also the year when an extraordinary combination of circumstances made it possible to broadcast the Fatima message, with its specific relevance to Russia, into Russia itself where it was to be heard by over forty million people.

This 'Fatima miracle' is the stuff of which legends are made, and has become part of the heritage of Aid to the Church in Need. José Correa, who works in the media section at ACN's headquarters in Konigstein, was one of those involved. The story really begins with the creation of 'Radio Blagovest', the unique Catholic radio station through which Aid to the Church in Need was able to reach the Ukraine and other parts of the USSR. It was through Radio Blagovest that the Ukrainian Bible campaign, mentioned above, was launched and it was this radio station which was to open up huge vistas for evangelisation across the USSR. José Correa had a walk-on role in the playing out of this extraordinary drama:

My own interest in Russia and the Soviet Union goes back quite a long way. I'm a Brazilian, and I went to Lithuania on a visit in the days when it was still Communist and the Church was being fairly savagely persecuted. Before I travelled there, I had been told about a particular family who were in trouble with the authorities – their son was in prison for his Catholic activities – and I very much wanted to visit them. I managed to find their home, but they were understandably reticent and wary of me. Eventually, when it had become clear that I was perfectly genuine, we went for a walk out in the forest where we could not be overheard, and I learned the appalling story of how this young man had been beaten and tortured – he was still walking with a bad limp – and discovered something of the everyday restrictions, humiliations, struggles and difficulties of life for Catholics in Lithuania.

Naturally, I wanted to do everything possible to help. What impressed me was their courage, and their absolute refusal to give up hope. They repeated what was also to be a watchword of Pope John Paul – that we should not be afraid. They were close to Nijole Sadunaite, who was a well-known anti-Communist dissident in Lithuania and something of a legend among Catholics there.

It was clear that one thing which would transform everything would be the possibility of radio broadcasts which would link them with the wider Church and help spread the Faith on a dramatic scale. I felt that this was something that I was called to do – that I must be their voice and get them the necessary help in the West. So I went to Konigstein, met Ton Willemsen and explained these ideas – and she had every right to regard me as simply crazy because I was just a lone Brazilian with a commitment to help people in a completely foreign country where I had no links at all. But the spirit of Aid to the Church in Need is extraordinary. If you can prove that you have a truly worthwhile plan, for the good of the Church, then all sorts of ideas become possible ...

Ton said that if I could produce a coherent plan for a Russian radio station within six months then I should come back to her with these specific ideas and she would get some action going. I went off and contacted everyone I could discover. I travelled to all sorts of places and had lengthy talks with all sorts of people, including some in Britain who were supporters of ACN and of other groups concerned with Russia. There was a lot of goodwill but at that time it just seemed impossible that a proper Catholic radio station to Russia could ever be achieved. No one had the real knowledge necessary, the contacts, the access to possible links within the country. Then – with just

one month to go before my six months were up, and
with flagging enthusiasm – I came across a lady in
Paris. Mrs Irina Albertino. I hadn't planned to discuss
the Russian radio plan with her at all. I had called on
her because someone gave me some parcel to deliver
to her and I dropped it in. But then we got talking.
Somehow, we got onto the subject of Russia and radio
broadcasts, and I told my story. She wept, and said
that she had been putting together plans for a radio
station that would broadcast a Catholic message to
Russia, but had simply lacked any funds. She was
already very much involved with Aid to the Church
in Need and was able to put the whole project to
Konigstein.

Irina was something of an apostle of Christian unity.
Baptised an Orthodox, she was later received into the
Catholic Church. She had worked as an assistant to
Alexander Solzenhitsyn and to Andrei Sakharov. In Paris
she edited *Russya Mysi* (*La Pensee Russe*), keeping alive
ideas of Russia culture and spiritual life. She worked
closely with Fr Werenfried and in the launch of Radio
Blagovest they were both able to realise some of their
greatest dreams. Irina – who died in April 2000 – was very
well known to large numbers of people who had been
persecuted for their faith and her message of reconciliation between Catholic and Orthodox was also of immense
importance both to Fr Werenfried personally and to
ACN.

When the radio broadcasts began, it was simply a
matter of beaming material from outside the USSR into
its territory, and then of receiving back letters and
requests for books, pamphlets, prayers, advice, and information. But events were now moving with extraordinary

speed. In 1991 Fr Werenfried went to Fatima. The USSR was now more open to the reporting of international events and news than at any time in its history. People in Russia were more aware of the outside world. Technology – starting with fax machines which by-passed the ordinary mail and therefore could not be subjected to searches or be tampered with – had outstripped the capacity and even the will of the authorities to ensure an ignorant and confused populous which would receive only the official Communist propaganda. There was a new mood. *Glasnost* had opened doors that could not be closed again. They were being kept open by the breezes whirling through them.

In a series of conversations that would have seemed quite unbelievable only a short while previously, the Soviet television authorities were persuaded to broadcast live the ceremonies from Fatima. Each October, huge crowds gather at the shrine in Portugal for ceremonies in honour of Mary. The year 1991 was to see the tenth anniversary of the assassination attempt on the Pope. He had long given Our Lady of Fatima the credit for saving his life. No one interested in the extraordinary Fatima story could fail to see the significance of his placing in her crown the bullet that had been meant to kill him. Now, on 13 October 1991 came a fresh Fatima miracle. The Russian television authorities agreed to co-operate with the broadcasting of a Mass from Fatima, which would include a sermon by Fr Werenfried directly aimed at the Russian people.

José Correa recalled later:

I can't describe the tension as all this was negotiated. Things were so delicate. All sorts of last-minute tensions arose, technological problems, difficulties

about which bishop was to do what at the ceremonies. You can't imagine – we had this miraculous
event on our hands, and we could hardly believe it
was happening, and at the same time it all seemed
capable of going wrong because there were so many
ridiculous things that conspired to block it at every
turn.

In the end, we had the sense that there was some
protecting hand over Fatima that day, which enabled
the broadcast to go ahead. It was almost as if there
was some sort of celestial war going on, and that in
the end the cause of God triumphed, but only after
the most narrow of margins, the breadth of an angel's
wing almost.

And so it was that Father Werenfried van Straaten, the
'cold war warrior' who for years had been pleading for the
cause of Russia's spiritual revival and had come to person-
ify the practical outpouring of the Fatima message
concerning the conversion of Russia, was able to speak to
the Russian people themselves. Some 40 million of them
listened, watching TV sets in their home, hearing for the
first time of a place in Portugal which had an extraordinary spiritual message which uniquely concerned their
own homeland.

'You are children of Mary, the best Mother that anyone
could imagine, a Mother who never abandons her children,' Fr Werenfried told his Russian listeners. 'And so
she, whom the faithful believers among your people
honour as Our Lady of Kazan and Patroness of Russia, had
already turned her Maternal gaze upon your fatherland
when, in 1917 in Fatima, she took up arms against Lenin's
revolution. This revolution was in the deepest sense a
total rebellion against God and hence a work of Satan.'

His message was that Mary herself was still pointing the way to hope – a way of conversion for Russia and for the West, the way of penance and of the Rosary.

Over 900,000 people were gathered at Fatima, and the Mass was being celebrated by Archbishop Kondrosiewicz, recently appointed as Bishop in charge of Catholics living within the borders of European Russia.

Two weeks after this broadcast Fr Werenfried launched his worldwide Rosary campaign with booklets and Rosaries being distributed across the world, specifically linked to the Fatima message. He was also shortly to launch a new campaign for Russian evangelisation, with great plans to work with the Russian Orthodox and to plan on a massive scale for the re-introduction of Christian teaching to as many people as possible through every possible medium of communication. The doors and windows of Russia were now open. As the last decade of the twentieth century began, the greatest challenges for Fr Werenfried and his movement looked as though they might be realised.

Chapter Thirteen

History was moving at an inexorable pace in Russia. *Glasnost* gave way to the complete ending of the Communist system – the collapse of the Soviet Union and the creation of a new 'Commonwealth of Independent States', apparent attempts by old-fashioned hard-line Communists to create a coup, thwarted by other factions and ending with a stand-off in front of the Russian Parliament building while the world watched on TV ... Gorbachev was sidelined and would find a new life as a strange world figure, lecturing and advising – Russia, corrupted by Communism, would plunge on from crisis to crisis, with shortages, political muddle, a powerful Mafia, and real economic power in the hands of Communist organisers who had been holding the reins of power for a long while and were best poised to ensure that they did well out of any new situation.

The evangelisation projects, planned and discussed in Konigstein and also in Rome slowly took shape. It was perhaps typical of Fr Werenfried that an initial over-enthusiasm got him into trouble. He wrote in the *Mirror* of a plan that had come into his mind – to give a sum of money to every Orthodox priest in Russia as a personal goodwill gift, so that these men could be used to spearhead a whole new evangelisation of this vast nation.

This backfired initially. Some people registered their

concern. To whom would Fr Werenfried be giving this money? Many of the Orthodox priests might be KGB informers, or outright supporters of Communism who had enjoyed a comfortable life while genuine Christian believers struggled under persecution. Why should Catholics, in any case, support an Orthodox Church which had traditionally been hostile to Rome? While these complaints came in – some from people who had themselves suffered at the hands of an Orthodox establishment for their Catholic or independent beliefs – events in Russia too conspired to make the plan seem unlikely to be realised. There was financial, social, and political chaos and corruption on a massive scale. Passionate nationalist groups had arisen, and were being manipulated by various factions. There was talk of new legislation to ban the activities of 'sects' – among which the Catholic Church was listed. The evangelising efforts of numerous Protestant groups from America, all of whom were anxious to go to Moscow to proclaim what they saw as a simple Gospel message which would make everything all right for everyone, caused tension and difficulty.

Fr Werenfried's original plan was soon modified: a sum equivalent to the money suggested would indeed be spent, but it would go to various specific projects on which Orthodox and Catholics could co-operate or which could be run by the Orthodox alone and involve necessary social action and primary evangelisation. This idea was radical, risky, and prophetic – and it worked well. It showed flair, imagination and courage, and brought in new supporters in the West who liked this ecumenical approach.

The needs in Russia were – and remain – so gigantic that the opportunities for work of all kinds is limitless. Clearly, support has to be given to the small and scattered

Catholic communities, to the restoration of such Catholic churches as exist – for example in St Petersburg – and to the bishops appointed to lead the Catholic faithful who live on Russian soil. Even this is fraught with problems. St Catherine's, the large Catholic church on the Nevsky Prospekt in St Petersburg – a landmark building in the city's most important thoroughfare – was gutted by fire in 1984. In 1992, after the collapse of Communism, it was handed back to the Church, but an enormous repair and restoration was necessary.

But many plans have come to fruition. An ambitious scheme to launch a chapel-boat, fitted out as a complete Orthodox church, to bring the Gospel message to far-flung regions where no church has functioned for years, was finally realised. Its team of Orthodox clergy now preach, baptise, teach and reconcile people to the practice of their traditional faith in large numbers. Meanwhile there are projects for youth work in some of the grimmest parts of Russia, including Siberia, where problems of drugs and alcoholism combine with a savage climate, a splintered economy, massive political corruption and a terrifying crime rate to create appalling conditions.

These were the projects that were to dominate discussions about Russia in Konigstein during the 1990s. But work in the rest of the world had to continue, too. In Latin America, Africa and Asia none of the projects funded could cease simply because there were new developments in Russia. Everything continued to expand.

Fr Werenfried, as the 1990s progressed, became a patriarchal figure, still in demand as a speaker, always telling audiences and church congregations that he was far from being a saint and begging them to pray for him, always raising huge sums in his 'hat of millions'. He was a forceful and still not always prudent promoter of new ideas. He could still get things wrong, still – by his own admission – be inept and tactless. He could infuriate people and his organisation could be a frustrating one for which to work. But he was an unmistakeably gigantic figure on the world stage of Catholic action.

Heartbreak and achievement, sorrow and courage, hope and disappointment, continued to play a part in the ventures with which Aid to the Church in Need was involved. Fr Werenfried was a welcome visitor to his 'Daughters of the Resurrection' in Zaire, greeted with dancing and singing and seeing at first hand their work among the local people and their infectious joy and enthusiasm. There was to be heartbreak here: at the end of the 1990s war swept over this land and in 1998 nine of these courageous and radiant young African sisters were to give their lives as martyrs.

In the West, Aid to the Church in Need had started to help groups associated with the pro-life movement, and Fr Werenfried often spoke about the evils of abortion and of the collapse of Christian family life centred on lifelong marriage. The horrors created by drug addiction were also something that ACN needed to address, and funds went to projects in Germany and in Brazil that were attempting to wrestle with this problem.

Fr Werenfried was a regular visitor to Rome. Always close to Pope John Paul II, he had audiences with him during which he could not only outline plans of work, but also discuss crucial difficulties that lay at the heart of the Church's mission: relations with the Orthodox, problems within the Western Church, the desperate need for new vocations and the best way to make use of the human resources available when confronted with the vastness of Russia and the huge opportunities offered in Eastern Europe.

Although a well-known figure and running a massive international charity, Fr Werenfried was not capable of acquiring the style and poise of a senior Roman cleric as he bustled about Rome. He remained somehow always the Bacon Priest, with a home-like and pastoral approach which never acquired the bureaucratic tinge or Roman polish of the career cleric.

José Correa recalled:

I remember one time when we were due to meet the Holy Father, and had been hurrying about Rome in the heat all morning. Fr Werenfried had taken off his Roman collar and left his shirt open at the neck to keep cool. We were sitting at a small café in Castelgondolfo, near the Pope's summer residence, where Fr Werenfried was due to meet him. It was good to relax and as we felt we had time to spare we all got talking. Then we realised time was running out for the appointment, so Fr Werenfried asked for his collar and made ready to hurry off. We couldn't find the thing! Not in his case, not among his papers, not in any pocket ... it had obviously been left behind at one of the places we'd visited that morning. Someone found a small white visiting card which, with a bit of adjusting, could be slotted in to the collar of his shirt to make an emergency Roman collar. He rushed off, fixing it into place as he ran. At the gates of Castelgandolfo we cried 'Turn round – let's see how it looks!' Just as well we did – he'd put it in the wrong way round, and there was the name – it was Irina Alberti's card as it happens – written across the front! We got it adjusted just in time ....

Fr Werenfried always remained at heart a priest,

concerned with people's pastoral needs. José Correa has
another anecdote:

> It was in Italy – we'd finally stopped for a meal at a
> place Fr Werenfried knew well. We'd both missed
> lunch and were hungry. When the proprietor came
> out he greeted Fr Werenfried warmly, but seemed to
> be not quite as usual. In conversation it emerged that
> he and his wife had had a series of disagreements and
> had decided on a divorce. That was enough for Fr
> Werenfried, who followed him into the kitchen.
> Neither emerged for a long while. Eventually they
> sent a message out that I should order some food for
> myself, which I did. I sat there alone for a very long
> time – it was dark and grew later and later. The
> restaurant was closed. Eventually Fr Werenfried
> emerged with both husband and wife and it was clear
> that a reconciliation had been achieved. By then it
> was very late and we had to drive on home. I don't
> think he ever got anything to eat.

Back in Konigstein there were always letters to answer,
plans to make, meetings to attend. The *Mirror* still came
out each month – and it seemed throughout the 1990s
that each edition had some still more amazing development to report concerning the collapse of Communism
and the future opening up of new possibilities.

And there were continuing echoes from the past. Back
in the 1950s, chapel-trucks had taken the Catholic faith
into the far-flung areas of where Catholic German
refugees from Silesia and Pomerania were living as
strangers in a new Germany and in territories where
there were no Catholic churches. There had been plans
for such trucks to swoop into Communist-dominated

144

Czechoslovakia and Hungary as soon as this became possible. Now, in the 1990s, a re-evangelisation was finally under way, but under very different circumstances from those first envisaged. Funds went to re-establish dioceses and equip parishes and seminaries. It was all that Fr Werenfried had ever dreamed – but fifty years later and with many difficulties that were making the new campaign much harder than an earlier one would ever have been. Yet there was another thrill to it as a new century beckoned.

The message of Fatima continued to be central to the work. In 1995 Fr Werenfried spoke of its significance:

> The Fatima message of the Mother of God was from the very start a blueprint for our campaign. In the past she helped us unceasingly to denounce the intractable evil of communism and support its victims, as Good Samaritans. Today she inspires us to share in the new evangelisation of Russia and to commit ourselves to reconciliation with the Orthodox Church. And she inspires us, likewise, to strive harder than ever for the conversion of the West which must precede the conversion of Russia.

His visit to Russia in 1992 produced an evocative moment, caught on camera. Fr Werenfried, wearing a massive Russian fur hat against the cold, and with one or two companions, went to the Kremlin where they stood in silence contemplating the great walls and praying the Rosary. No one else was present except, extraordinarily, two nuns. They came over and joined in the Rosary. Some one took a photograph. It was the moment that was perhaps the culmination of a lifetime's work. Here was the last 'cold war warrior' praying Mary's prayer at the heart of what had once been the core of the atheistic communist regimes which threatened to engulf the Church.

During that 1992 visit, Fr Werenfried visited Moscow, St Petersburg, and Novgorod. He had a meeting with Patriarch Alexei of the Orthodox Church and announced the 'new Dimension' of the work of Aid to the Church in Need, joining with the Orthodox for the new evangelisation of Russia.

Two years later he was back on Russian soil, this time to visit Siberia and Moscow. He had another meeting with Patriarch Alexei and they got on well. Plans were now going ahead for all sorts of projects.

The two boats, funded by Aid to the Church in Need, which now travel slowly up and down the Don and Volga rivers, cover the area of Volgograd, formerly known as Stalingrad. There are plans for further boats. The story of the chapel-boats has been made into a video, shown at Catholic parishes and schools and to Catholic organisations in the West. Scenes of people being baptised, of tinkling bells summoning congregations to prayer, of golden onion-domed turrets moving serenely downriver on the top of this miniature church, evoke fascination. It is a story unimaginable in the 1950s, and a sign that God will produce unexpected ideas to meet new challenges.

'He is always the priest,' José Correa recalled after a trip to Russia with Fr Werenfried. 'We were in a Russian hotel when a Dutchman came up and asked "Are you the Bacon Priest?" Fr Werenfried was delighted to meet a fellow countryman and they got talking. It turned out to be providential. This man had been away from the Church for a long time and wanted to make his confession. They found a quiet place, there in the hotel bar. It's as if all the time, there is some work that Fr Werenfried can do.'

As the 1990s ended, it was inevitable that there should be some speculation about the future. The year 2000 saw him still busy with plans, working on his autobiography, praying for Russia, praying for the Daughters of the Resurrection in Africa, writing in the *Mirror*. But he was getting old and frail. There had been a number of serious illnesses in his life. Now, after a series of strokes, he is confined to a wheelchair.

I visited Konigstein in September 2000. It was golden weather, and the little town was enchanting. I spent the days working on material from the archives, interviewing members of staff, consulting the photographic library, viewing video footage showing all sorts of activities funded by the charity. Pottering around the town, I found the graves of Bishops Kaller and Kinderman in the cool graveyard of the old baroque church. In the early mornings I walked in the beautiful hills around the town – there are enchanting views – and hurried back for breakfast where I would join others: Daughters of the Resurrection with mellow African-accented French, busy staff members about to hurry off to meetings and appointments, Ton switching easily from German to French to English as she chatted to different groups of people.

Aid to the Church in Need had decided to show itself to the local people; for twenty-five years it had been headquartered among them, but many of the residents of Konigstein knew little or nothing about the work of the charity or the role it had played in local post-war history. A 'Day of Open Doors' was planned for the Saturday: a large marquee was being erected, beer and refreshments had been ordered, trestle tables were being stacked ready for use. In the main entrance a large display was being created showing the history of the work, going right back to the earliest days: photographs of children in refugee camps, maps showing the Iron Curtain, early fund-raising posters. Up and down the stairs arrow signs were pointing to different departments, where work would be on display: laminated posters were showing aid projects in different countries and continents. The hard-pressed staff were a little harassed, getting everything ready. It looked set to be a big event.

One evening I joined Fr Werenfried and Ton for dinner in a neighbouring village about fifteen minutes' drive from Konigstein. This has been their home for the last twenty years. There are two adjoining flats in a pleasant modern building, with a balcony looking out over the valley and mountains, and with the lights of Frankfurt glittering in the distance. A team of nuns – nursing sisters – now looks after Fr Werenfried during the day. After a lifetime of talking and preaching, arguing, begging and organising, he is now silent for long periods. As Ton prepared supper and we watched the evening light over the scene below us, I thought of all the times I had been with Fr Werenfried – as he led hearty evening singing sessions during a weekend conference for ACN promoters, or preached magnificently in Westminster Cathedral, or was a guest at a talkative dinner in London, or presided at a meeting in Rome or a conference in Konigstein. Always, his large personality created a buzz, got people talking, and made things happen. Now there was a stillness, a sense of rest. He was happy to answer my questions – still speaking fluent English with his strong Dutch accent, and still with a flash of humour from time to time. But everything was at a slower and more measured pace. We looked over at the hills: lights were coming on in the spick-and-span prosperous homes that nestled pleasantly amid the green landscape. It was hard to imagine a different Germany – hunger and ruins, refugees and the brutality of conquest and fear. We talked about the changes that had taken place over the decades.

Over supper Fr Werenfried spoke about his family. Photographs of them are on the wall of the room where, until very recently, he used to say Mass every day. The altar still stands there against the wall, but he cannot use it any more. Now he can no longer stand, and says Mass seated at a low table.

In the sitting room, a large Polish suit of armour stands by the door. It was a thank you gift from Polish Catholics. Around its neck have been casually tossed some of the various medals and orders with which he has been showered over the years. There are orders from Austria, from Germany, and from Holland and Belgium as well as from various Catholic institutes and organisations. All around the room are books and gifts from the places he has visited. There is a large toy pig for the Bacon Priest. Above one bookcase hangs a remarkable carving from Africa. It shows a bad confession. On one side the penitent is kneeling, but he is being dishonest, and his guardian angel weeps. On the other side, the Devil laughs gleefully, knowing that he has a soul waiting for him.

The room, with its large windows and shelves of books and mementoes, is pleasant and home-like. Newer additions – the wheelchair, the walking-frame, show the owner's age and frailty.

We'd spoken of many things – about his brothers, about the girl he might have married, about the changes in the Church and in Europe during his lifetime, about the state of things in Holland, and in Germany and in Britain. He'd spoken a little about the way he had made clumsy or tactless mistakes over the years. We reminisced about people who had worked for Aid to the Church in Need in Britain: Philip Vickers, Sister Catherine Shakespeare,

Alex Tomsky, Kevin Grant. We'd talked about places he'd visited, about various meetings and conferences where he'd spoken. I remembered him congratulating me when I was engaged to be married – and reminded him that was a long time ago and that I'd now been happily married for more than twenty years. The work goes on. There are new projects all the time – in Russia, in Africa, in countries where there are tensions with Islam. And Fr Werenfried's prayers for all of the projects continue. After his first stroke, he was told he should take exercise, and he used to walk through the nearby fields, praying the Rosary – getting some strange looks from passers-by! Now, he prays at home – always asking that God will provide for the work to continue, and always – as he admits publicly – admitting his own failures, and asking for forgiveness, and for protection for the work with which he has been entrusted for over half a century.

We talked about some of the latest projects. He has been a speaker at Family Congresses, held to promote the Christian message on the importance of family life. He has given great support to conferences run by Human Life International, opposing abortion and euthanasia. He has spoken at big youth events and at congresses run by new movements in the Church such as 'Communione e Liberazione' in Italy. The work in Russia goes from strength to strength. A chapel-truck is now planned for the districts of Yekaterinburg and Orenburg in Russia, for prison visiting and bringing the Orthodox liturgy to people who would otherwise never have any spritual help in the winter months. And there are still personal landmarks: most recently the sixtieth anniversary of Fr Werenfried's ordination, celebrated with a great Mass at S'Hertenbosch Cathedral in his native Holland attended by members of his extended family and a vast circle of friends and co-workers.

Finally I asked him if there was one thing he would want me to say in any book I'd write about him. Was there any one message he was keen to convey? He gave me a long and steady look and answered slowly but unhesitatingly: 'Always have a great trust in God. This is the one important thing. You must always have great trust in God.'

Aid to the Church in Need is a Catholic charity supporting over 7,000 projects every year in Eastern Europe, China and throughout the world.

For more information about the work, please contact your National Office:

UK
1 Times Square
Sutton
Surrey
SM1 1LF
Tel: 020-8642 8668
Reg. Charity No. 265582

IRELAND
151 St Mobhi Road
Glasnevin
Dublin 9
Tel: 01-83 77 516
Reg. Charity No. 9492

AUSTRALIA
P.O. Box 6245
Blacktown DC
NSW 2148
Tel: 02-9679 1929
ABN 62 418 911 594

USA
378 Broome Street
New York
NY, 10013-3706
Tel: 1-212 334 53 40
ID number: 95-319 4083

CANADA
P.O. Box 670, STN H
Montreal, QC
H3G 2M6
Tel: 1-514 932 0552
Reg. Charity No. 130362593 RR0001

Index

Index